Seeing Another Way

Changing Perspectives. Changing Lives.

Roger E. Breisch

Published by Dancing With Chaos

Cover design: John Arends
Book Design: Kevin Moriarity

ISBN: 979-8-234-13718-0

This book is dedicated to the thousands who, over the 75 years of my life, have helped me See Another Way.

Contents

Preface

"Everyone's going through something."

I talk to high school students, and when I remind them, most nod in agreement. Perhaps not in this moment, maybe not even in the recent past, but everyone suffers. The human journey is not easy. "It's not meant to be," I suggest. "We gain some of our greatest wisdom during moments of hardship." But, until we can see those moments as teachers sent to help us reimagine the world, they can cloud our view and make the world, and our lives, seem dark and foreboding.

When we are in their grip, it can seem as if life's challenges will haunt us forever. However, they pass, just as day follows night, and sunshine is always on the heels of stormy weather. Pain, suffering, and heartache seldom last. I have asked many people who have suffered if they would change the past to avoid the pain. Often, they say they would not because of the wisdom they gained.

This book contains stories of hundreds of people, myself included, who have come to see pain, suffering, and even desperate confusion, in new ways. "Seeing Another Way," I call it.

Based on my seven plus decades, few people see themselves with precision. We do not see accurately because the human brain, as magnificent as it is, ignores most of the world around it. We are bombarded by an enormous amount of sensory data: auditory, visual, olfactory, taste, touch, and emotions. No human can take in everything they encounter. If we did not ignore most of what assaults us, we would become paralyzed. So, we make sense of the world based on the bits and pieces we don't ignore. The world we end up believing to be real and accurate is always incomplete and imperfect.

Even our self-image is based on a partial view of who we are. I ask people, "Are you, at least at times, overly self-critical? Do you say things to yourself you would never say to another human being?" The response is usually overwhelmingly, "Yes!" We create a self-portrait based on negative self-talk, and miss, or dismiss, the many positive things others see in us. A more accurate, and typically more beautiful, portrait is warranted…and available if we just look.

The image on the cover is a metaphor derived from a conversation more than 15 years ago with a high school student who told me that when she looked in the mirror, she hated everything she saw. Whenever someone expresses such a sentiment, I ask if there is anything about themselves or their life they appreciate. Most everyone will offer something on which to develop a conversation. But this young woman told me there was nothing she liked or appreciated. I asked if she had friends at school. "I am blessed," she told me, "I have many wonderful friends." "If I asked them," I inquired, "what would they tell me about you?" She paused, and very quietly said "They would tell you I care about them a lot!" So, I proceeded to ask:

Roger: "Do you love them?"

Young woman: "More than you can imagine."

Roger: "Are you kind?"

Young woman: "I often fail, but I always try to be."

Roger: "Are you generous?"

Young woman: "I would give anything to anyone, if they needed it and it was in my power to give."

I reminded her that, regardless of what she sees in the mirror, her friends see love, kindness, generosity, empathy, and compassion. She thought about that for a moment and said,

"Thank you so much! That really helps. I forget to look at myself through the eyes of people who love me."

This book is all about seeing another way. Since the way we see the world is always incomplete and imperfect, the people who know us and love us see a more complete picture of who we are. That portrait is one we need to acknowledge, honor, and embrace.

For whom is this book intended? It is for anyone whose spirit feels tattered. I've selected stories for this volume that can help people see their lives in new ways and witness the wisdom available to them.

It is also meant for anyone trying to help a friend or loved one who is suffering. We all have the power to help others see themselves in new ways. But here are three caveats.

We live in a culture that wants to fix problems, even others' problems. Since we are generally uncomfortable being with others who are in pain, we are desperate to fix them. The first caveat is we need to remember we cannot fix another human being. They need to fix themselves. We need to learn patience. With time, dwelling in pain can often offer wisdom.

The second caveat is that what you believe does not matter. Your solutions will not work for another's unique situation. Stop ending sentences with periods. By remaining "in the question," unexpected paths forward just might appear.

The third caveat, if we stop ending sentences with periods, is to use only authentic questions. Authentic questions are those to which we have no answer, and any answer is acceptable. There will be times when we simply cannot help. That, too, must be acceptable. The guilt that can accompany such a "failure" is real, but it is not a reason to redouble attempts to fix.

I have authored this book to help. It is not my attempt to fix others. It is meant as an encouragement for those in pain, and those trying to help. Regardless of the depth of life's challenges, it is always possible to see them another way.

I hope these stories help.

Roger Breisch
June 17, 2026

Introduction

"Do you think the pain I am feeling is my heart trying to find its way back into the world?"

Even though I was gifted with these twenty words many years ago, they remain etched on my soul. They came from a young caller to a suicide hotline I was answering that fateful afternoon. His heart was wrenched by a decision he had made that would hurt his family. After a lengthy conversation, this vulnerable, kind young man found the courage forgive himself. He came to understand he had made the best decision he could have at the time. He began to see himself in a new, more compassionate way.

I have been blessed by astonishing wisdom discovered through more than 11,000 conversations answering depression and suicide hotlines over 20 years. I had the extraordinary opportunity to witness the transformations that often occurred as people, through authentic and vulnerable reflection, began to see themselves in new, more loving, ways.

However, these pages do not only contain stories of callers to suicide hotlines. I have been gifted with encounters in many corners of my life in which wisdom became apparent and abundant. I participated in a teen leadership program called "Operation Snowball." At its heart, Snowball is a program for teens who wish to live healthy lives—lives in which drugs and alcohol remain at bay—and to meet others who share their vision. Whenever teens feel safe, and discover an opportunity for authenticity and vulnerability, their lives open before us brutally and unadulterated. Stories of abuse, neglect, unrelenting bullying, battered self-images, drugs, alcohol, and so much more appear unbidden. In those moments, as well, I have come to understand courage, strength, and resilience in new and profound ways, wisdom only accessible from the depths of our suffering.

For eight years I was invited to write an essay in a bi-monthly community magazine. Since I was given great latitude regarding the themes and stories about which I wrote, there were many times in which chance encounters with fellow citizens would alter the lenses through which I viewed the world.

< >

When asked about the next phase of life, after leaving my last full-time job many years ago, I generally replied "I'm seeking my vocation." As it turns out, my vocation had been in search of me, but I was deaf to its call. Vocations, I have come to understand, can be patient and persistent.

Experiences on the suicide hotline crept into my writing, thinking, and activities, but I never wanted, nor intended, to become "the guy who talks about suicide." It felt somber and terrifying. How could talking about suicide, especially teen suicide, bring anything other than grief and sadness?

Then, shortly after I retired, a local bank invited me to speak to their senior account holders. They were interested in several essays from my blog; especially one entitled "A Time I Will Not See." In it, I wrote how each of us will gain some measure of immortality through the messages our lives leave imprinted on youth. They will carry some of what they witness in us into a future we will not see. In my remarks at the bank, I backed gingerly into the topic of teen depression and suicide.

At the end of those remarks, one elderly gentleman—heavy-set, gruff, and wearing a baseball cap—pulled me aside. As tears welled up, he told me his grandson had recently ended his own life. Looking forlornly at the floor he continued, "I never saw it coming." The unspoken words written unequivocally on his face asked, "How could a grandfather not have seen that in his grandson?" When I explained he was not alone, teens often hide their deep sadness, it seemed to alleviate his overwhelming guilt in some small way. When I asked if I could give him a hug, tears returned, and we shared an embrace.

I began to speak to more senior communities, but instead of treading softly, I started by revealing that the young people they know and love—grandchildren, great grandchildren, grand nieces and nephews, and others—are at risk. Between the ages of 15 and 25, suicide is often the second leading cause of death. It surprises nearly everyone. I explain the multiple trends and issues that make a young life difficult, and the countless reasons young people remain cloaked in silence, including fear, embarrassment and confusion.

Because of my experiences, several high schools have asked me to speak to their sophomore health classes, when they delve into the difficult topics related to mental health. The teachers find that stories from my work help students in their relative innocence. They discover they are not alone. The teachers tell me the teens find the stories meaningful and memorable. I use the "Words in Red" exercise you will discover later in this work, to help them understand that their image of self is often an incorrect and incomplete vision of who they are, and who they can be.

So, I come face-to-face with my vocation. Frederick Buechner once said, "The place God calls you to is the place where your deep gladness and the world's deep hunger meet." I am "the guy who talks about suicide." The devastating consequences of self-chosen end-of-life are a powerful wakeup call. As a result, I am called to use my experience in all corners of society, but especially within groups known to be at higher risk of suicide and suicide ideation: teens and seniors. Teens are at risk because they are inexperienced in the pain, heartbreak, and challenges of being human. Elders—I prefer "elder" to "senior"—are at risk because they so often feel pushed aside, useless, and hopeless. In attempting to build bridges between elders and teens, I speak honestly with elders about teen depression and suicide and implore them to help in the battle to slow the onslaught amongst teens. When I do, a flame of hope arises with the thought that, maybe, just maybe, there is a vital role for them yet to play.

Seeing Another Way

After finishing my master's degree in mathematics, I was invited to teach at a private, preparatory high school. Since I was only a few years older than many of my students, I often felt inept…unpolished…incapable of reaching those who struggled mightily with algebra, geometry, and trigonometry. When you fail in many endeavors, there is often a remedy. When you fail as a teacher, your students live with your ineptitude until the day they pass from this Earth. They needed a guide with great patience, and I often felt I came up short. Those failures weigh heavily more than 50 years later.

However, a note left on my website, reminded me of moments in which, perhaps, I was less inept. I was touched by the memories it evoked. The missive was from a man who arrived from Iran his junior year in high school and went on to become a college professor and dean. I could present him as proof of my success as a teacher, but he would have excelled with any teacher. While he worked diligently, he had an innate aptitude for mathematics. He and a few of his peers easily opened their minds to the concepts behind the numbers and theory.

Despite their innate ability, I remember one or two moments when he and his friends came with a question, standing on the precipice of understanding, but not quite over the edge. In those moments, we would engage with the mathematics. When understanding eluded us we would ask each other if we could see the problem another way. As we challenged each other to look anew, contest each other's assumptions, there would come a moment when their eyes—or mine—would light up as we completed a critical neural pathway and a new piece of the puzzling language of mathematics fell into place.

I had no idea how central to my very being the idea of seeing another way would become. So much of my time on the National Lifeline entailed deep and intimate conversations in which I would encourage people to examine the assumptions they held about themselves and their lives, and see a new way forward.

Questioning our self-image

I have come to the conclusion that people generally see themselves inaccurately. I wonder if most people do not know who they truly are; see themselves as less than who they are or can be. We believe we see and understand the world around us, and even our own world, with remarkable accuracy. What if we do not?

Nowhere is this more evident than with callers on a suicide hotline.

A teen who called was in desperate need of healing and self-absolution. Since he was wracked by disabling, deforming disease, the ensuing bullying from both peers and self, demarcated a life of failure, pain, and self-loathing. And yet, every story he recounted from his brief life spoke of his caring, generosity, and fierce defense of loved ones. Late in our time together, I asked him to describe something, anything, wonderful within. "I can't," he told me in a soft voice. "I hate everything about myself." I recalled the many stories of caring, generosity and love he recounted only moments earlier. I asked if he could witness, not shortcomings, but his huge heart. "It's your superpower," I suggested. I also told him I loved him, and who he is in the world. Near tears he told me those were words he seldom hears. "Would you be willing to see your life through your enormous heart?" I asked. "Thank you, I will try," he told me just before the call ended.

Past traumatic events, unfortunate mistakes, and painful emotions often take on undeserved significance. The goodness, kindness, and compassion of the past are lost in the face of overwhelming heartache. People share the harsh and tragic nature of the human journey; their pain so palpable I could feel it even across vast distances. And yet, so often, when people looked at their lives anew, to see events, actions, and feelings in new ways, the pain would ease in small but significant ways. Often, amid their revelations, out of the darkness and heartbreak, erupted astonishing wisdom.

Hidden Wisdom

Why, I wonder, if there are precious vanes of wisdom and insight available to us through suffering, do we keep it hidden in the corners of our lives? Depression, anxiety, suicide ideation, and suicide surround us every day. How do we manage to live lives in which these very human maladies seem rare and obscure? Most of us have never inhabited the depths of despair—moments during which pain is so severe that ending life, even knowing the grief and confusion it will cause others, seems the only way forward. And because the experience is so foreign, we are frightened by it. We become paralyzed by the fear that we could become trapped in similar horrible thoughts and moments. We do not have answers to our own confusing and grief-laden questions, how could we even begin to understand the depths others face? In those moments, fearing we may become engulfed with no way out, we give advice, and run, returning those moments to the recesses where we hope they will remain.

After remarks to a service organization, one member spoke up. "Two years ago, one of our members, a person we all thought led a happy and wonderful life, chose suicide." "What," she pleaded, "could, or should, we have done to help him? The ensuing sense of loss, grief, and guilt has been so difficult." Two other members of the club approached to express concern for grandchildren who were suffering horrendous bouts of depression and suicidal ideation. "What can I do or say," they both pleaded, "to save someone I love so dearly?" I look them in the eyes and am witness to their pain and fear. My answers always feel inadequate and seldom still the roiling waters. I take some solace in knowing that, often, our presence and support is the most valuable things we can offer.

I wish such requests were abnormal; aberrations in the course of the work I have chosen in the years following my time on the suicide hotline. Sadly, they are not. After speaking to students at a local high school, one sophomore approached to tell me her best friend ended his life a few weeks earlier. She ended up in tears and in my arms. In any group, when it is revealed that I have spent time with thousands who have contemplated ending their lives, there is almost always at least one whose life has been altered by a self-chosen end-to-life.

In this work, I attempt to scratch at the surfaces, claw at bits and pieces of our grief and confusion. The ensuing pages will not end the confusion, but suggest that life's challenges are, in many ways, answers in and of themselves. They come unbidden and leave us with wisdom and understanding we never knew possible. They are the teachers for which we yearn but never knew existed.

Part 1 contains narratives of my interactions with others during which our mutual view of the world has been altered. In Part 2, I take some time to reflect on the many lessons I have learned over the course of my life. Neither of these are complete renditions of the encounters and/or lessons learned, but they have bubbled to the surface as I have contemplated what to share with the world.

< >

Please know, I understand the importance of privacy, especially surrounding the heartbreak that emerges from living a human life. The stories in this volume are real stories. Many of them are told as they happened with permission from the person involved. Those for which permission is impossible to obtain, I have altered and removed enough detail to make them opaque, to leave the person behind the story with privacy and anonymity.

One final thought. Over these many years, people suggest that the professionals and paraprofessionals who answer depression and suicide hotlines save hundreds or even thousands of lives every year. My response to those sentiments is that we do not save lives. We are, however, given the incredible gift of spending time with thousands of people who find the courage to save their own.

Before we begin in earnest, there is a topic essential to the very idea of seeing another way. While I am not an historian, I have a suspicion about human history. I wonder how far we might have come if it were not for *homo sapiens'* ability and desire to be inquisitive. How many of the dramatic turns in our species' evolution came about because someone simply asked "What if?" If, as I soon will suggest, we have lost the ability to assemble the most intricate and complex questions, are we lost?

In the coming pages, you will discover many of the insights that erupted from my numerous encounters came as a result of a timely and challenging question.

The Essential Nature of Questions

"It's a life thing. It's a political stance. It's not just a vehicle you are using to help people find their voice. The notion that the questions are more important than the answers is a stance."

Peter Block[1]

Fresh out of college, I taught in a private high school in New Jersey. As faculty advisor in the dorm, I began each day at breakfast with the students. One freshman would frequently catch me in the dining room. "Mr. Breisch," he would intone, "may I ask you a question?" I would turn and say, "You just did! Would you like to ask another?" At the time, our early morning repartee was nothing more than a way to point out a bit of irony that that student seemed unable to grasp. I now believe he was pointing me towards my future…a future in which life's questions have become infinitely important, and answers more harmful than constructive.

So, even though we are not in line awaiting breakfast, may I ask a question? Or two? Have we lost the art of assembling provocative words into questions that inquire into the great mysteries of the Universe? To what extent do the answers we summon imprison our thinking and hold it hostage? When was the last time you heard a question so profound it left you in awe of its far-reaching implications…wanting to learn more…or simply with a moment rife with new understanding? How often, in the face of questions, do we find ourselves in search of the nearest convenient answer, regardless of its ability to add a bit of wisdom to the human narrative? How often do we formulate questions for which we truly have no answer, as

---

[1] From an interview I conducted with Peter Block in March, 2001

opposed to those whose sole purpose is to allow us to let loose a carefully crafted declarative response?

My father would say I was often wrong, but *never* in doubt! In conversations with my wife and children I find myself too willing to jump in with a statement ending in a period; a very large period at that. I wonder how our lives might have evolved differently if, when faced with a thought I found difficult to accept, I might respond with "That's interesting. Would you tell me more?"

Over the years, because of a unique position I held near the center of many community debates, I have listened, as many issues traveled the highways and byways of our public discourse. Regardless of the time, residents always find themselves amid debates about the future of the community and its surroundings. As I listened, I was always struck by the dearth of sentences that end with the extraordinary question mark. Our "public hearings" were too often attended by people who have stopped listening. I only wish we were becoming better listeners, but, alas, our public discourse has become ever more contentious; our listening skills having atrophied.

The word "discussion" itself calls into question our intentions. Its evolution from Latin meant to "smash apart" or to "scatter and disperse." Shouldn't our conversations begin with an intention to gather our ideas in a generative fashion rather than scatter and disperse them?

In the coming years, humanity will face moral and ethical issues more profound than any we have ever faced. Brain scans will allow us to know what others are thinking, thus obliterating even the most intimate forms of human privacy. Genetics will allow us to design our children. The harvesting of human organs will blur the line between life and death.

These deeply challenging issues will require new ways of seeing. Unless our answers are preceded by the most profound questions we can conjure, I fear we may be forever lost.

So, it will come as no surprise I have come to appreciate the remarkable value of the critical and underused question mark. We have a multitude of punctuation marks at our disposal. Periods are, by far, the most frequently used. Exclamation marks are essential for expressing emotion. Commas are necessary for understanding, and apostrophes allow us to leave out letters and/or numbers and to show possession. But in my experience, our failure to use question marks, in both written and oral narratives, leads to massive confusion, agonizing misunderstandings, and excruciating disagreements. In the case of suicide ideation, a dearth of questions can lead to the end of a person's life.

Imagine for a moment, your own life has become so fraught with pain, both physical and emotional, that you have come within moments of ending yours. Your life, as you know it, has ceased to have even a remote sense of meaning. In one last grasp at survival, you call a friend, loved one, or even a suicide hotline. Then, in the ensuing conversation, what you receive is an onslaught of sentences that end in periods:

"You can't be thinking of suicide."

"Your life has so much meaning."

"So many people love you."

"Think of the lives you will damage or destroy."

"You are such a good father."

"You are so smart." "Creative." "Hard-working."

"Caring."

"You are so beautiful."

When facing a person in trouble, because we feel afraid and helpless, and because we live in an action-oriented culture, it is easy to fall into the trap of problem solving—and the oft used tool in that toolbox, declarative sentences.

A person who is lonely, depressed, or even suicidal, needs a non-judgmental ear and empathy. Sentences that end in periods, especially those that can be heard as intimidating or threatening, come off as judgmental, rehearsed, obligatory, hollow…even vulgar. If the person on the receiving end does not argue verbally, a voice of denial will surely begin to scream in their head. All we have managed to do is foment an argument…and add guilt to the already endless list of emotional hurdles the other person faces.

If, instead, we end our sentences with the little-used question mark, any response provides an opportunity to agree rather than argue.

"What feels the worst in this moment?"

"What do you think you might do now that might help, even in some small way?"

"If you have felt this way in the past, have you discovered things that have helped?"

"What do you think the people who love you would want for you right now?"

"Is there something—anything at all—that you cherish about yourself, something positive you bring to the world?"

Any positive response to those or similar inquiries opens the possibility of a life-affirming conversation, and leaves feelings of guilt or denial on the outside looking in.

After a long call on the National Lifeline, when the caller said she felt better, I asked what in our conversation helped. "You just asked questions. It was wonderful."

People who have reached out because life seems worthless, futile, or even vile, want, more than anything, to be heard. They want to know that others care. How do we show we care? We care when we are deeply interested in the messy, confusing, chaos that defines another's life, not in finding solutions. If we are truly interested in understanding rather than solving, the only way forward is with the extensive and generous use of the "squiggle above a period": the delightful question mark.

If you are ever with someone who believes their life is stripped of any shred of value, and you respond with, "You are so caring and kind," or "You are so smart and creative," a voice of denial in them will build an impenetrable wall that screams, even silently…

"How could you possibly know?"

"You don't understand *my* life!"

"You are just being polite."

"You have to say that…you're my mother."

From that moment, the two of you are on opposite sides of an argument; one you do not want your suicidal partner to win.

A simple, yet powerful question, one I have used thousands of times with people who tell me about the difficulties of their life, is "Would you be willing to tell me more?" Then I just *listen.* With Intensity.

Authentic questions open the future to new possibilities. Declarations—sentences that end in periods, especially those that make clear no future exploration of possibilities is welcome—end discovery.

Some time ago, I received a call from a friend as she drove from her home to a friend's home several hours away. Tess' friend was seriously considering suicide. Tess was frightened and felt woefully unprepared. She was hoping for some counsel in the hours it would take her to reach her destination. We spent considerable time discussing the power of questions.

I asked her to pause whenever she felt the need to declare a "truth," and to take the time necessary to translate her declarations into sincere and authentic questions.

There are abundant questions that can open the future to new possibilities, as you will read many in the coming pages. Another question that I have come to love and use generously is: "Is there something, anything at all, that you love about yourself?" Often, after a pause, a person will quietly admit something.

"I care a great deal about others,"

"I love to write poetry,"

"I am a hard worker," or

"I still have a great deal more to give."

With any admission of value, even if it seems a delicate, fragile thread, instead of any argument, you have agreement…and solid ground on which to build a future.

Tess, bless her, spent several days with her friend, using the power of questions to help her friend choose life. The following week, she called me and said, "turning periods into question marks was lifesaving."

What is an authentic question? Simply, it is one for which we truly do not know the answer, and *any* answer is acceptable. A friend once reminded me that an authentic invitation is one to which "No thank you," is an acceptable, and appreciated, response. If I ask a question and find myself mulling a rebuttal, I must ask myself if my inquiry was an attempt to understand, or merely an opening to state a position. If so, no one on the other end of that conversation is going to feel heard.

When trying to help another, our inquiries can elicit silence or refusals. This, too, must be acceptable. The most generous thing we can do for another is to respect their reluctance and let them know we care and are here for them whenever they wish to speak about whatever topic in which they wish to engage.

As we move through the coming stories, I trust you will come to appreciate the power of authentic questions.

Part 1
The Journey

In the course of seven and a half decades, thousands of people, events, and conversations have had a profound effect on the way I and those with whom I connected, began "Seeing Another Way." In Part 1 of this book, I share some of the most significant. You will meet people of all ages, races, careers, and sexes who, because of our interaction, chose to see themselves and their lives in new ways. Along the way, I too, have had my life altered.

Chapter 1
When Our Hearts Break

Early in my tenure on the hotline a young man called and began our conversation with a dire warning. "I have a gun in my lap, and when we're finished talking, I intend to use it." With little experience to bolster my confidence, it was a terrifying moment.

Answering calls on a suicide hotline is extremely rewarding even though the work is demanding, intense, and often frightening. Over the years, and through thousands of conversations, I came to understand there is astonishing wisdom only accessible during times of pain and heartbreak.

This person's life and sense of self were defined by abuse and exploitation. He had been abused in every imaginable way, and the assaults came at him from all directions. Now, in his early twenties, he felt used and useless…his life had no value. There was nothing left to do but end the anguish. "I have a gun in my lap, and when we're finished talking, I intend to use it."

In *any* conversation, veering in the direction of our own choosing, risks leaving others feeling insignificant and unseen. When speaking with someone who is contemplating suicide, remaining focused on them is not only generous, it can also be lifesaving. As a result of a long and intense conversation, I began to understand the depth of his hopelessness, and we built a trusting relationship. So, I asked if I could share a story from the Hasidic tradition. He accepted my invitation.

As I recall the story, a disciple asked his Rebbe why the Torah tells us to write holy words *on* our heart. "Why doesn't it instruct us to write them *in* our heart?" The Rebbe said it was quite simple. "We write the holy words on our hearts, because, as we are, our hearts are closed. So, we write them *on* our hearts, and there they stay, until, one day, our hearts break, and the holy words fall in."

After recounting that tale, I asked that anguished young man how many times his heart had been broken. He admitted it was impossible to count. I told him I wished I could take away his unfathomable pain, but I was helpless to dull even the sharpest of its edges. *That should never happen to a child!* However, knowing his heart had been shattered hundreds of times, I asked if he learned anything about the human journey that would enable him to help others. "Have there been holy words that have fallen into your heart?" I inquired.

I was stunned by his reply.

He told me story after story of his ability to save the lives of other young men who were suffering the kind of abuse he experienced. Only he understood the depth of their pain. When he began to grasp his incredible capacity for empathy, and his ability to save others, he told me he put the gun away. While life had stolen his childhood, he began to see, in return, it left him with a huge, compassionate, and empathetic heart.

I would not wish that kind of pain and heartbreak on anyone, let alone a child. And yet, there is wisdom available only in moments of darkness and heartbreak. That paradox leaves me suspended in the middle of a horrific dilemma. If we eliminate pain and suffering, we potentially lose access to profound wisdom. When I address teens, as I am often privileged to do, I suggest, even if your heartbreak is over the loss of a beloved pet, or because a close friend moved away, wisdom infiltrates your heart, and it grows. Ever after, you are better able to comfort a friend or classmate who suffers a similar loss.

None of us craves heartbreak. No one wants to feel the pain and grief of losing those closest to us. And yet, those are moments few of us can slip past unaltered by the pain. When my father died, I remember thinking that grief and heartbreak is the price we pay for love. Those are moments when truly feeling the deep sense of loss, experiencing all of it and its tentacles in our lives, gifts us with wisdom about the human journey. Grief and loss are teachers we need for our hearts to grow and enable us to understand the pain others can, and do, endure.

Having spent many hours answering calls on depression and suicide hotlines, I learned that helping those who suffer is some of the most life-affirming work any person can be invited to do. On the other side of suffering is a profundity of joy and wisdom unavailable to us without the journey into the depths.

When our hearts break, holy words do, indeed, fall in. We learn something important about the nature of the human journey. In moments of heartache and pain, if we are open to the lessons, we gain in our capacity for kindness, generosity, empathy…and love. Our hearts grow in those moments, and we are unexpectedly more human, not less. We are broken open, not broken.

When we hide suffering, we concentrate it in hidden worlds. We send the elderly to retirement and nursing communities; the infirmed and disabled are sent to homes. Depression and mental illness are closeted behind the closed doors of professionals. And while these places are caring and wonderful, people on the outside forget the suffering that exists behind those doors. By concentrating anguish into places of caring, those left to deal with the suffering are overwhelmed by the enormity of what we ask of them.

When suffering is hidden, we are left believing it is not normal for humans to suffer. This is exacerbated today by social media. So many callers to the lifeline compared their lives to the lives of friends, forgetting that most people only tell of their joys and successes. Their pain and heartache are seldom uploaded to the Internet. Those who suffer cry in silence, believing it is their unique frailty or weakness that leaves them in pain. We think, "Since others around me are doing well, perhaps it's just me who is weak and unable to cope with life." We miss suffering's doorway into understanding and sagacity.

How might the world be different if every person were to find ways to allow human suffering to reinfuse their lives. What if we began with the courage to let the world see our own vulnerabilities, bringing the reality of the human journey back into our lives and communities. What if each of us spent time in places where we have gathered great suffering and gave a moment of respite to the caregivers who are becoming overwhelmed?

To affirm life, we must affirm *all* of life…including suffering. We are bereft of wisdom, empathy, and love when we go to great lengths to eliminate or hide suffering; we do everything we can to avoid the journey that eventually leads to an understanding of the fullness of the human journey. It is in our moments of pain that gifts of gratitude and wisdom become available.

We live in a culture that wants us to believe suffering, even risk, can be made optional, or, if not, at least veiled and secreted away. Anything that reminds us of our mortality, recalls the fragility of our lives, and is sequestered. We are flooded with images and products that hint at the prospect of everlasting youth…and an end to suffering. When we do suffer, we wear carefully crafted masks behind which we hide, lest others learn of our weaknesses and failures. Those who find themselves in crises are often deserted by friends who are frightened by the prospects of their own mortality.

We know, at a very deep level, much of humanity's most profound wisdom has come from individual and collective suffering. Recall how Joseph Campbell taught us the value of the heroes' journey…the descent into the Nether worlds, only to reemerge, imbued with greater humanity and wisdom.

< >

I am reminded of an experience with teens at Operation Snowball one Thursday evening. Two teens provided us with a fascinating and enlightening experiential exercise. They divided us into two groups. The first group, the one to which I was assigned, shared memories of positive life experiences. The second shared less pleasant experiences, ones we would rather not recall. When finished, we reflected on the differing atmospheres that emerged in the separate rooms. As you can imagine, those differences—everything from tone of voice and interaction to body language and emotions—were dramatic.

As we talked, we noted how much more energizing it was to be with the group sharing the positive aspects of life. We agreed that we prefer to spend our lives with people who are positive and enthusiastic rather than those who wish to dwell amid life's challenges and crises. It was a wonderful exercise.

My concern is how those lessons inform our lives. As much as happiness, pleasure, and times of joy are wonderful places to find ourselves, life is false and unreal when we try to wring sadness from its midst. There is an ever-growing arsenal of pills and medications offering ways to annihilate sadness. Please do not misunderstand; having spent 4,000 hours answering a suicide hotline, I know that medication can turn a life that is unbearably difficult into one that is contributory and fulfilling. The medications available to us can truly be lifesaving.

But let us be careful not to confuse deep depression—for which medication can be vital—with life's tragedies and sorrows. While we love being together in joyous ways, anyone who has been with others who share pain with authenticity and vulnerability, knows the intense connections we make in those moments. When I tell others of the uncountable joyous moments during the 55 years I shared with my father, they learn something of who I am. But when I reveal the tremendous pain and heartache—the deep sense of loss—I experienced when he died, we become connected in a much deeper way. I learned something new and deeply profound about myself having lived through the experience of his death—the raw and harsh way life is often lived through us. It is in moments when you allow me to see what drops you to your knees in agony that you reveal something about who you are that cannot be revealed in any other way. Then, and only then, can I look into your eyes and say "I know you. I understand what you love about life and what you value." Then, you can feel truly seen.

While moments of joy and happiness are irresistible, when we show up in the vulnerability of pain, sadness, and agony, we show up more authentically and more capable of love. And, when we can be with others in their most intimate, painful moments—without the need to fix them or wrest the pain from their lives—in those moments we most powerfully show up for one another.

As I bring these thoughts on the wisdom available from moments of pain to a close, here is a note I wrote to a young woman at Operation Snowball. She approached me one Thursday evening to tell me of a deep sadness that infused her life. We spoke briefly, but the appropriate words eluded me in that moment. The next morning, I sent her the following note.

Julia,

Let me begin by telling you how touched I was that you reached out to me last night. I feel blessed by your invitation. At the same time, it feels as though, in the moment, I was unclear and inarticulate. I have reflected on our time together and would like to share some of those reflections.

The deep sadness you described is indeed difficult. When we are in that place, we wish so much to be free of the pain. I have spent hundreds of hours on the suicide hotline with people who are trying to escape the gulf they feel in their lives. In those moments I will often ask, "Is there something you are learning from this pain that helps you better understand the human journey?" The typical response is "You have no idea!" When our hearts break, the holiness of the human journey enters it in a new way and our hearts grow. In those moments, we become more able to help others on their journey.

It is sometimes helpful to think of all the emotions that populate our lives—sadness, joy, anger, fear, etc.—as passing clouds. They come into our purview, and whether we want them to stay or not, they pass away. It is the definition of being human. The journey is to notice them and see what they have to teach about being human. If we view them as teachers, we also see each as a gift. We can be thankful for them…and not grow attached to them. They will go…and one day return to teach us yet again.

You are an amazing gift in the lives of so many. Your joy, kindness, the love you share, changes each of us for the better. You inform us in your own unique way, about the miracle of the human journey. As long as you continue to grow into the extraordinary young woman you are becoming and are willing to let your life speak to others, then let the sadness simply evaporate. That cloud, too, will pass.

Finally, this morning as I was reflecting on our time together, I was reading The Book of Joy: Lasting Happiness in a Changing World, *a conversation between His Holiness the Dalai Lama and Archbishop Desmond Tutu. Two quotes from that volume inform this missive. The first was from a psalm: "Who passing through the veil of tears makes it a well." When we allow tears and sadness to break open our hearts and enlarge their capacity, we become a well from which others can gain wisdom and strength.*

The second is, "And so I would say to everyone: You are made for perfection, but you are not yet perfect. You are a masterpiece in the making."

When I looked deeply into the eyes of the extraordinary young woman in front of me last night, it became clear to me that you are a masterpiece in the making. I am blessed by you in my life.

Hugs,

Roger

Chapter 2
The Power of Connection

One Thursday night at a weekly Operation Snowball gathering, a young woman I had come to know well during her first two years in high school was in a corner of the room alone and looking forlorn. I walked over to say hello, give her a hug, and asked how she was. She said she was okay, as teens will, even if life is a challenge. Then, when she asked how I was, I looked her in the eye and said something I had never said to a teen prior to that night: "I'm better now that you are here." We hugged again and I thought that was that.

When we nudge the world, even in insignificant ways, we can change the course of human history.

Many people are aware of the Butterfly Effect: a butterfly flapping its wings in one part of the world, over time and distance, can alter the weather in a distant land, often radically. However, few people know the origins of the term, and its originator deserves credit.

> *In 1961, (Edward) Lorenz was using a simple digital computer to simulate weather patterns by modeling twelve variables, representing things like temperature and wind speed. He wanted to see a sequence of data again, and to save time he started the simulation in the middle of its course. He did this by entering a printout of the data that corresponded to conditions in the middle of the original simulation. To his surprise, the weather that the machine began to predict was completely different from the previous calculation. The culprit: a rounded decimal number on the computer printout. The computer worked with 6-digit precision, but the printout rounded variables off to a 3-digit number, so a value like 0.506127 printed as 0.506. This*

difference is tiny, and the consensus at the time would have been that it should have no practical effect. However, Lorenz discovered that small changes in initial conditions produced large changes in long-term results.[2]

Even seemingly insignificant changes in any moment can produce tsunamis of changes over time and distance. If this idea changes how you think about what you do in the coming moments, it is possible the future has just been altered.

At Snowball, in addition to weekly Thursday night meetings, there were two 3-day weekends each year. The staff strove to make these events a safe place for teens to speak with authenticity and vulnerability about their lives. I was always stunned by the unexpected stories of sadness, anxiety, abuse, depression, and suicidal ideation that erupted from teens I thought were happy, safe, and content. Over the years, I heard so many cases of abusive relationships, sexual assaults, addictions, abandonment, and so much more, I wonder if anyone lives a life as simple as my own.

During the weekend, the events on Friday and Saturday culminated on Saturday night with an event we called "It's a Wonderful Life." It is a panel of 4 or 5 teens and an adult who tell, often amidst oceans of tears, the story of their life. With as many as 160 teens and adults in the audience, we need an abundance of tissues placed strategically through the room.

We had such a weekend not long after I affirmed that young woman by telling her, "I'm better now that you are here." To my surprise, she was a participant on the "It's a Wonderful Life" panel. As soon as she began, she revealed that her home life had become exceedingly difficult, through no

---

[2] Gleick, James (1987). *Chaos: Making a New Science*. London: Cardinal. p. 17. ISBN 978-0-434-29554-8.

fault of her own. She was so heartbroken, she told us she began to consider ending her life. Amid her remarks, she looked at me and said to the participants, "One of my worst days was a Thursday not long ago. I considered skipping our evening meeting but decided to go anyway. When I arrived, Roger gave me a hug, and when I asked how he was, he said, 'I'm better now that you are here.' In that moment I knew I mattered. My thoughts of suicide evaporated."

I had known this young woman for more than two years, and knew her to be strong, resilient, and courageous. I do not believe for a moment, lacking my affirmation, she would have ended her life. But, if she proceeded into a world in which initial conditions—her understanding of her self-worth—were altered in even a small way, the course of human history shifted. She has gone on to obtain a degree in environmental engineering and will change the world for the better.

< >

Educator, philosopher and author, Neil Postman, once wrote, "Children are the living messages we send to a future we will not see."

I love any opportunity to speak with elders—people who have lived long enough to gain a deep appreciation for life's complexities, intricacies, and convolutions. When I use the term *elder*, I refer to people who have been through the depths and reached the mountaintops that are part of every human journey. Having lived through lows and highs they become wisdom-keepers; they have learned and lived the values, morals, and ideals of the culture.

I speak to elders because the young people they know and love—grandchildren, great grandchildren, grandnieces and grandnephews, and others—are at risk. Between the ages of 15 and 25, suicide is often the second leading cause of death. The question I am often asked is "Why?"

There are myriad answers, but a serious and dangerous trend is the disconnect that exists between those I call life's apprentices and its masters. In ancestral times, children learned to navigate day-to-day life from their parents, but they learned wisdom from their grandparents. In indigenous tribes, the elders told the stories of the tribe, and through those stories they passed along the ideals, principles and values held most sacred.

I have thought a great deal about why we learn day-to-day life from parents and wisdom from grandparents. I have asked many people, "If your life was falling apart, would you tell your parents?" Most people will pause, look at me sadly and say, "No, probably not." Why not? Perhaps it is because, of all the people in the world, the ones from whom we most want love and acceptance are our parents. How frightening, even subconsciously, might it be to go to them and admit we have failed, have made a terrible mistake, or have let ourselves, and by implication, our parents, down. When children fail, parents can rely on an automatic response to fix, when what is most needed is a listening, non-judgmental ear. The dynamics are fraught with minefields of emotion and misunderstanding.

Grandparents, removed from the responsibility of day-to-day guidance, know the immeasurable value of simply listening, loving, and affirming. It would be impossible for me to recount the times teens were brought to their knees by the pain brought about by the loss of a grandparent.

Unfortunately, we have, too often, locked away our elders, offered them golf clubs, and said, "Don't call us, we'll call you." After speaking to a group at a beautiful community in Las Vegas, when I came to the end of my remarks, one resident looked at me sadly and said, "Please do not misunderstand, I love it here. I have friends, the staff are wonderful, and I am cared for. But now that my family knows that they do not visit anymore."

We are all in need of the wisdom held by our elders. When life becomes challenging, when we find ourselves in despair, there are those who have been where we are, and know that challenges are survivable and that there is often joy and wisdom on the other side. When I speak with elders, I will recall conversations with teens who tell me they lost the love of their lives. "You don't understand," they will say through tears, "I will never love another as much as I love the person I just lost." Not to make light of the pain these young journeyers are experiencing, but elders will often smile and even roll their eyes. "Oh, I remember that!" they will say. "How wrong I was."

I love to ask elders if they can change the course of human history. Some believe they can, many believe they cannot.

My plea to our culture's wisdom keepers is that they gently and generously reassert their influence into the lives of young people. "Share your wisdom. Share your stories. Tell of life's joy and happiness, but also share its difficulties, its heartbreak, and its grief. Let them know that wisdom flows from suffering, and that in its aftermath, life can be, once again, joyful and life-affirming."

After one conversation with elders in another beautiful retirement community, one resident admitted he had contemplated suicide in his middle years. "I've written a great deal about that," he told the group. When I asked if he shared his story with his children and grandchildren, he repeated a phrase I have too often heard: "Why would I burden them with my problems?" "*Because they need to know!*" I responded. "Your grandchildren see you in this beautiful place and think you skipped through life without ever having a care in the world. Then, when they struggle, they conclude they are uniquely weak and incapable of navigating life. It would be an incredible gift for the young people in your life to learn that grandpa suffered and still lived a long and valued life. Might you, by sharing *all* of your journey, change the course of their lives…and hence that of human history?"

At another engagement, I was on the schedule of events as an "inspirational speaker." One resident plopped down on a chair right in front of me and asked, with a wry smile, "Are you going to inspire me?" I laughed and told her she could decide when I finished. When I finished speaking, she looked at me and said, "I am *so* inspired! I often feel, at my age, that it is time for me to go. But, listening to you, I remember I am the matriarch of this family, and I am going to reclaim that role. I want to remind my grandchildren that I love them and am there for them." A woman sitting just behind her, raised her voice and said, "My husband and I did not have any children, so we do not have grandchildren. However, I have many grandnieces and grandnephews. I am going back to our apartment this afternoon, get their addresses, and send each of them a note that simply says, 'Remember, I love you.' "

After one presentation, an elderly gentleman said, "My grandchildren know I love them…I send them a check every birthday." That broke my heart to think that, in his view, sending a check rather than sharing wisdom, represented love.

In an era of decreasing interpersonal connection and increasing focus on screens and technology, the eldest among us know better than most, the power of compassionate conversation. After spending thousands of hours counseling teens in leadership forums and on a depression/suicide hotline, I know how influential elders can be on future generations. There can be a special relationship between our oldest and youngest generations—one that can energize, heal, and inspire.

Every time two people form a deep connection, each of them is altered. And, as Neil Postman suggests, every time we alter a life, especially that of a young person, a piece of us lives into generations yet unborn…and the course of human history is forever altered.

Chapter 3
Nudging the World

"I am done. I cannot take it any longer." she said. "I've suffered from depression and anxiety since I was a teen, and I simply cannot do it any longer."

This call arrived years into my tenure on the hotline, so I was not surprised by its beginning. It was how the call ended that took my breath away.

We spoke for a long time about the challenges she faced. The more we talked, the more inadequate I felt. The depth and complexity of her struggles overwhelmed me, as it did her. I struggled to find helpful words. When speaking to others, especially about their struggles, it is critical to search inside for what I am feeling and be honest with callers. "I'm having trouble finding words that might help," I told her deep into our conversation.

A few moments later, she told me about a conversation with her counselor. "She believes every person has a purpose. Once I find mine, she thinks I will feel better. But what if I don't believe every person has a purpose?" she asked. I admitted I was not sure that was true either. "Here's what I do believe," I told her. "Each of us can nudge the world every day. Everything we do, every moment we help another human or improve the environment, nudges the world ever so gently in a minute new direction. Hundreds of times each day; millions in our lifetimes. And, if you believe in the Butterfly Effect[3], those gentle nudges will change the course of human history."

"That was it," she said. Fearing I might have said something inappropriate, I confessed my confusion. "What do

[3] See the Chapter 2

you mean?" I asked. She responded, "A few moments ago, you admitted you were struggling to find words to help. Well, that was it. I don't need a purpose more than nudging the world hundreds of times every day. Perhaps that is enough. When I called, I was on my way home to self-harm. Now, I am determined not to."

Even years later, as I write these words, that moment takes my breath away and tears emerge. I never know how calls may or may not change callers, but I will forever know how they change me. Every call left a unique trace in my heart, and that one certainly did. In thousands of previous conversations, I had never used the words that came to me as I spoke with her. Why, I wonder, was I given them in that moment?

I have reflected frequently, since that moment of connection, on the idea of nudging the world. That idea was meant not only for her, but for me as well. Having long sought a deeper understanding of my own life and its meaning, those words spoke to me. They told of the value of small deeds—nudges—done every day. In those moments when I rue not having done something "big" with my life, those words console me. To echo the caller, perhaps that is it.

< >

A war rages within. One of the most deeply troubling cultural convictions is the belief that a human life is valuable when defined by "big" accomplishments. The bigger the impact on humanity, the more valuable a life is. We celebrate that belief every day in newspapers, magazines, and narratives that go viral on social media. What if it is not big accomplishments that most alter the future the world, but the ways in which we support others.

A young scientist called one afternoon. He was desperate to change the world through his work, but, as hard as he tried, he could not find a position to help him continue his studies. Every position for which he applied was given to a person with more experience and superior credentials. He always came up short. He was certain he needed to be "the best" to make the mark he desired to make. If he could not be the best, he told me he could not go on. The doubts and fears were so overwhelming he told me he had given up and was finding it hard to find the motivation to do anything.

During our call, he mentioned that playing the violin gave him comfort when he was stressed. I asked how often in the past month he had been paralyzed because he was not the best violinist. He was puzzled by the question, but after a pause replied, "That would be about zero." "And yet, there are thousands of violinists, who are not in the first chair in their orchestras, but make a necessary, invaluable contribution. So, even if you never occupy the first chair in neuroscience at some institution, is it possible you could make invaluable contributions?" The question took him by surprise and seemed to remove a huge burden. He ended our time with a renewed sense of purpose and told me he was prepared to continue his quest.

I think about nature and how we, as members of the species *Homo sapiens,* are outliers among the millions of other species. I do not think a bird dreams of "big accomplishments:" building a new kind of nest, applying technology to allow for more space, room for other families, or to create nests that last twice as long as those built last year. A bird discovers twigs, leaves, grass, and other bits of nature and places them one at a time, making thousands of small contributions until, one day, a nest emerges, just like those built by its species for thousands of years. A beaver, likewise, builds a dam the same way thousands of ancestors built theirs, nudging the world one twig, branch, or log at a time. We, as humans, strive to make the future better by making it different, altering it radically.

There is an arrogance in believing I know what is best for the future. I want to always remember I make the world better, change the course of human history gently, and perhaps most profoundly, by nudging it one smile, one kind word, one friendly gesture at a time.

What if a life is valuable regardless of the size of our "accomplishments"? What if it is valuable simply because the one who lived it nudged the world in innumerable ways? And, since I list my title as "Speaker Provocateur," allow me to be provocative. What if nudging the world is enough?

Chapter 4
Others Before Self

There is a recurring story on the Lifeline, and it sounds like, "I am exhausted, weary to the bone. I have done so much for so many other people, and now, when I am desperate for help, no one is there for me. I feel deserted."

I remember one caller for whom this was her story. She felt alone and deserted by family and friends, and was in so much need of support, she said she could simply not go on. Often, when I was unable to uncover a reason for a caller to persist in the face of despair, I would simply ask, "In spite of your pain and loneliness, is there a reason why you want to live?" This caller simply said, "I have so much left to give."

It is hardwired into human DNA to be generous. Whenever I speak with people who are overwhelmed and exhausted by a life of giving, the most productive and life-affirming path forward is always, paradoxically, to give even more. Others before self.

A young woman, despite suffering from anxiety and clinical depression, found herself in a caring, loving relationship. She admitted she never thought she would find someone as loving and generous as her current partner. However, she was riddled with guilt about the difficulties he faced dealing with her frequent afflictions. "I am not good enough for him. He deserves so much more. I need to end our relationship," she told me holding back tears.

I asked if she felt her partner struggled to deal with her issues. "He says he loves me, wants to be with me, and understands what he is facing. But he deserves more. I need to leave. He will be happier if he finds someone who is easier to be with." "So, you will give up your happiness in a loving, caring relationship so your partner can be happy?" I asked. "Absolutely. That is the least I can do if I love him." she responded. I continued, "Moments ago, you suggested you are not good enough for him, and yet, you are willing to give up your own happiness for his. Is it possible that that alone is proof you are more than enough? Despite your own struggles, your first thoughts are for his happiness rather than yours." "I hadn't thought about it that way. Let me think about that some more. Thank you," she said as we ended the call.

I spoke to a young actor, who, because he was having trouble finding work, began to doubt himself as a thespian. Now, even though he had helped innumerable others, no one was there for him in his hour of need. As his story unfolded, he described a recent, successful theatrical project he led in which more than fifty people found gainful employment. I came to appreciate this young man's innate sense of the importance of relationships and his ability to create community. It was clear that, at his core, he was "other-centered." It came as no surprise that, because others are his priority, caring for himself seemed selfish. He often felt self-hatred when he focused too much on himself.

I am careful to use appropriate language when talking to callers, however, there were moments when I simply could not help myself. As we talked, his self-confidence grew as he realized his true power erupted, not from acting, but from compassion and empathy for others, and his innate understanding of relationships and community. He told me there were people in his life who, believing his success lay in his thespian talents, would say "You're going to be great someday." He told me he resented those remarks since he had already given so much to the world. As we both came to understand his real talents lay elsewhere, I suggested he look at them and say, "Fuck you...I'm great right now." "You know what, you're right!" he said. We both had a good laugh as his self-doubts eased ever so slightly.

< >

I grew up in a world in which LGBTQ+ would have been nothing more than a strange concatenation of letters. I lived my formative years at a time when the incredibly complex issues of gender and gender identity existed as they do today but were unspoken. I have come to know and love many people who are represented by LGBTQ+. I hope to always be an advocate for acceptance and understanding.

I say all this as prelude to a call I received from a young man struggling with acceptance from his family over his chosen career. He was a successful drag queen. He was so successful he was able to support his extended family by performing around the world. Despite his generosity, he felt a lack of familial acceptance and was so distraught he was considering jumping from the upper floor of a building from which he was calling.

Unconditional acceptance of callers is essential if there is any hope of connection. As the call began, because of the sheltered life I led, I feared I would fail this young man. While I can relate to hundreds of professions and careers, his was totally foreign to me. I had never even met a drag queen. I felt hopelessly unprepared, certain I would never find words to help.

It was immediately clear this was a person who yearned for acceptance, that of his family, but most importantly with acceptance of self. I heard in his voice that, despite all he had given to others, he felt, somehow, his life was not enough.

His life was so much more than enough. As we spoke, I discovered a place of generosity within him that changed the course of our conversation. Whenever and wherever he performed, because of his renown, young men who wished a similar career looked up to him. He always took time to encourage them in every way: from perfecting aspects of their performance and wardrobe, to helping them find the courage and self-esteem to follow their dreams in a culture that rejected them. "Do you see what your life is really all about?" I asked. "Can you see how you are making the lives of so many others better because of your kindness, love, and generosity?" As we spoke, I could hear the strength in his voice and the meaning of his story growing. My admiration of this young man and his desire to change the lives of others also grew.

Those few moments of intimate conversation changed both of us. He was touched by the acceptance and affirmation I offered and my perspective of what he offered the world, and I discovered an ability to pierce my personal veil of prejudice and peer into the humanity of a young man's love, empathy, and compassion.

Years ago, I listened to a series of lectures entitled "Questions of Value," by Dr. Patrick Grim, professor of Philosophy at the State University of New York at Stony Brook. It was a remarkable twelve hours. One of the profound questions he explores is what makes for a valuable life. He concludes that such a life is, at its core, admirable, and surrounded by a shell that is enviable. He goes on to say that the challenge for so many whose admirable core dominates, is that that core never seems enough. No matter how much they have given, there is more to give. I remain humbled by thousands who, through their lives, have shown me there is always more to give to others before self.

Chapter 5
Death as a Spiritual Teacher

"I simply can't return for the rest of these sessions," she declared. "People have *no idea* what death really means. They talk in such generalities and abstractions. My first-born son, Jason, died in a car accident a year ago. I can tell you what a death really feels like."

I once facilitated a series of dialogues entitled "Death as a Spiritual Teacher." At the end of the first discussion, Kathy approached. She was sad, disappointed, and even a bit angry. Her emotions overtook her as she told me about the death of her son. My heart broke. Then I pleaded, "It is because of your experience that having you return to the dialogue is critical. Please help us understand."

Because of the advancements in medical science, infant and childhood mortality knocks on the doors of far fewer families than even a hundred years ago. We do not know the grief of burying a child. Those who do, like Kathy, often suffer alone.

Kathy did return to our discussions, and we became friends. I learned the true meaning of grief when she and I sat down to record and publish an interview about the death of Jason. For hours I listened. I felt her overwhelming grief. For hours we shed a tsunami of tears together at her kitchen table.

But that is not the end of Kathy's story. Jason's death was the beginning. Kathy, feeling very alone in her grief, for an entire year following his death, could barely leave her living room. But then she did. She not only left, but, feeling Jason's presence in her life ever more profoundly, Kathy went back to school, earned her doctorate in psychology, finished her residency 3 months after turning 60, and spent several years working for the VA helping veterans deal with the horrors of war. Then, still feeling Jason's presence, she was called to Boston to offer what she could to help still the raging waters of the opioid tsunami.

I would give Jason back to Kathy this moment if I could. But a part of this deeply wise and caring human being would be lost to us. Whenever we find ways to circumvent suffering, parts of our humanity slip away.

One morning, as I walked along a bike path near my home, a fundraising 5K race was in progress. A block or two later, I came across a man handing out information and answering questions. I stopped and asked about the nature of the event. He explained that he lost his young daughter to a rare fatal disease. He was raising money to help end the scourge. I recall thinking, as with Kathy, that this young father must feel alone in his pain since so few could ever understand the depth of his heartbreak.

Do I want to return to the days when we must bury many of our children? Absolutely not! My wife and I have two grown children, and I am thankful we did not have to bury either along the way. But if we had, would I have a different relationship with the fragility and value of human life? Of that, there can be no doubt.

Then, too, what about our desire for immortality? What would it mean if medical science found ways to reverse the natural process of aging, enabling us to live significantly longer, or to live forever? Alternatively, what of the so called, singularity: the point at which computer technology and artificial intelligence expand exponentially with the hope that we can be uploaded into a remote sector of cyberspace and "live" forever?

These ideas leave me with a plethora of thoughts, questions, and fears...and frightfully few answers.

What of the preciousness of each day, if an infinity lay ahead? How many people today, on their deathbeds, remind us to take advantage of every moment, and make sure we tell those in our lives that we love them, lest we lose the opportunity? If there were an infinite number of days, would we heed that advice? Would we even understand it?

What wisdom, stemming from the loss of loved ones, would humanity be willing to forsake? How might the world be less if Kathy had not lost Jason? How many veterans would not have had her wise and caring counsel? How many lives would we have lost to the opioid crisis? Am I suggesting that Jason's death is somehow justified by the wisdom, love, and generosity she shared with others? Of course not. But Jason's death nudged the world in new directions, and his mother taught me a great deal about life.

Homo sapiens is unique among species in our desire to build wealth; accumulate more than we need. Whenever I venture into the woods, I marvel at species that take what they need and give generously of what they have to every other species in the astonishing web of life. We take more than we need and give the smallest sliver with great trepidation; fearing that giving away wealth is a zero-sum game. And yet, the more we accumulate, the less we appreciate what we have.

Why, I wonder, would accumulating additional days of living be any different? At the extreme, with an infinite number of days in our quiver, what makes us think we would aim our arrows with care rather than abandon?

Shortly after the AIDs epidemic coursed across the globe, before the introduction of protease inhibitors that would save his life, I met a man who was HIV positive. I asked how his diagnosis, a death sentence when first received, changed him. His response? "It gave me a sense of identity—not necessarily in a good way—that I was a dying person. I was going to live life to the fullest. We can all learn from the specter of death, the wisdom of the elder. For me, the issues were, take care of yourself…take care of your relationships…be kind."

Jack London once said, "The proper function of man is to live, not to exist. I shall not waste my days trying to prolong them. I shall use my time."

I will too, knowing the time I have left is precious and short.

Chapter 6
The Courage to Acknowledge Our Goodness

Another recurring theme on any crisis line involves callers who are unable to see their inherent goodness.

I spoke one afternoon with a young man who was struggling as he neared the end of his high school career. In junior high school, life opened a gorge before him that included skipping school, poor grades, alcohol addiction, and "friends" who were horrible influences. He fell in and was held captive. Two years into high school, not wanting his life defined by the choices that caused his fall, he found the courage to claw his way out of the abyss. He got off the drugs and alcohol, eliminated the bad influencers, returned to class and compiled a strong academic record in his remaining two years of high school.

One of the miracles of the hotline is that callers, desperate for help, will allow me an unadulterated glimpse into their heart and soul. This young man certainly did. I was witness to a young man defined, not by failure, but by wisdom, courage, and fortitude. And while his magnificence was so clear to me, all he could see were the mistakes that led to his trip into hell. He was blind to the miraculous nature of his recovery. I was in awe of his courage.

An hour into our time together, I paused and said, "I do not say this to callers, but I love you, young man. I am in love with who you are, and who you are becoming through the struggles you have faced, and the courage you found." In that moment, he began to cry. "Why the tears?" I asked. He paused and said quietly, "It is not because I am sad. I am crying because you are the first person I can recall who ever said they loved me." In that moment, I found it impossible to hold back my own tears. How could a young man preparing for college, never have heard others tell him he is loved and lovable?

I have used, with thousands of people in hundreds of audiences, a simple exercise.

I ask people to look at the following list of words and choose two, three, or four they would use to describe themselves.

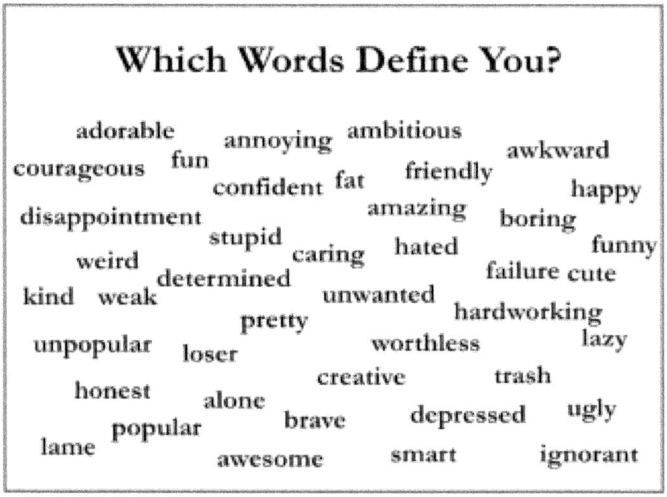

Once people have done that, I will ask, "Now think of people in your life who know you and care about you—someone I call a truthteller. Imagine two, three, or four words *they* would choose to describe you."

When people have done that, I ask, "Even if the two lists you just created are different in some small way, who has two different lists?" Everywhere I go, regardless of the demographics, at least half the people, sometimes everyone, will acknowledge differences. Why is this so pervasive?

The reasons are many, but the most prevalent one arises because of the negative descriptors I call "Words in Red."[4] People will often choose them in their self-description. Those who know us and love us typically will not. We overemphasize the mistakes of our past, forgetting that all humans make mistakes. Those who know us and love us, understand mistakes happen, and judge us less harshly than we judge ourselves.

That high school senior, given an opportunity to choose from the list of descriptors, would have chosen words like disappointment, failure, loser and worthless, because he was still so focused on his mistakes and failures earlier in his life. I, on the other hand, believing his mistakes led to his resurrection, would choose words like courageous, hardworking, determined, and ambitious.

It is not the mistakes we make that define our character, but how we feel, and what we do as a result.

A call came from a young man in a parked car. He was unmerciful. "I am a horrible, evil person. I don't deserve to live." I asked if he would be willing to share the events that led to such fierce self-condemnation.

He had just left a store and was sitting in his car, overwhelmed with anger and self-loathing. Moments earlier, he became frustrated in the checkout line. When his frustration got the best of him, he lashed out at a woman in line behind him, letting loose hurtful comments. He was deeply disappointed and judging himself unmercifully. "It is not the person I want to be. How could I have been so cruel to that poor woman. I hoped I was a better human being than that," he explained near tears. What I could hear was his fear that

[4] In my TEDxQuincyStudio remarks, the positive descriptors are blue and the negative ones are red.

unreasonable, unrestrained anger defined him. "This is the kind of thing I won't let go of for weeks," he admitted.

He was a veteran; I was shocked to hear details of what he witnessed while he served his country in a war zone. I cannot even imagine how I might view the world differently had I lived through the horrors he recounted. Now, he was trying to create a post-military life. He was struggling in a relationship and stressed by his job and mounting bills. He had no relatives or friends who could understand what he was going through. He felt alone. He was living his entire life "on the edge."

When he told me again that he felt himself a horrible, evil person, I asked, "Do you want to be a person who is humbled and sorry, vowing to try harder next time, or would you rather be a person who dismisses his actions and doesn't care?" Now in tears, he admitted the depth of his sorrow and how he was determined to try harder in the future. "So, while you disappointed yourself a moment ago—did not live up to the code of conduct you expect of yourself—in this moment, you are living into your highest expectations." He paused and whispered, "Yeah, I guess I am."

"Is it also true," I pressed, "that you learned from this painful experience? If something similar happens in the future, can you imagine being more gentle, kind, and loving?" "Absolutely," he said. "So, are you a wiser, kinder, and more generous human being than you were even a few moments ago?" I asked. "It never occurred to me to think of it that way," he confessed, "but maybe I am."

Before the call ended, I told him I grieved his self-doubt. In the brief time we spoke, I had come to know him as a man who wanted so intensely to be perfect. "I am sorry for the mistake you made. Both of us wish it had not happened. But here is the dirty little secret about being human," I told him,

"You will err again! When we fail, and rue the error, it is evidence of our humanness…not our inhumanity."

< >

A young man in his twenties had fallen off the wagon so many times, and disappointed so many people, he could not go on. He hated himself for his numerous failures to remain sober, which he blamed on personal weakness. "I have seen others find the courage to make it through. Why can't I?" he asked with a voice tinged with self-hatred. I reminded him that failing was indeed unbearable, but getting back on your feet and trying one more time is a sign of determination and strength, not failure and weakness. "You have a disease," I reminded him. "Failing many times is, unfortunately, part of the road to recovery for those who suffer from addiction."

I asked when his most recent drinking began, and how long he had been sober prior to that. He told me he started drinking only two weeks earlier and was sober for six months prior to that. After congratulating him on six months of sobriety, I asked if he liked the sober version of himself. He told me he liked that person and was proud of him. I asked if he thought he could find that person again. I heard a surge of confidence in his voice. "Yes, I'm quite sure I can."

< >

When I was thirteen, my family visited the New York World's Fair. There is so much I remember: seeing New York City for the first time, standing in front of Michelangelo's *Pietà* (its first trip outside the Vatican), the Unisphere, General Motors' Futurama, Disney's "Audio-Animatronics" and so much more.

However, an experience deeply etched in my psyche was the ride through Pepsi's salute to UNICEF and the World's Children. Created by Disney for the Pepsi pavilion, "It's a

Small World," subsequently became a permanent ride at all the Disney theme parks. The ride did make it seem like a small world—seeing so many places and cultures in just a few moments. What was beyond anyone's imagination in 1964 was the extraordinary way in which the world would shrink in the ensuing years, particularly with the advent of the Internet.

A friend discovered a university student who had written on Facebook about ending his life. She suggested I send him a friend request. "Perhaps the two of you could chat," she suggested. Moments later we began to do exactly that on Messenger. We talked about the difficulties of his life and why he was considering ending his. All the while he kept asking why I was wasting my time on him. "I am not worth it!" he repeated.

After typing for an hour, I suggested it would be easier if he called me. I was unprepared for his reply: "I would sir, but I live in Pakistan, and I cannot even afford cigarettes."

I realized in that moment that an aging American and young Pakistani were communicating across cultures, thousands of miles, and three generations about what it means to be human. No matter the place on the globe, nor our age, the human journey is the same.

I fell in love with this young man's wisdom, kindness, and generosity. In part he said to me:

> *"I am specializing in English Literature but have been a student of comparative religions, philosophical logic, parapsychology, metaphysics, ethics, and general philosophy. People tell me I am weird because I read so much. I don't like stupidity, but I encounter it everywhere. Not many people understand me because they are stuck in trivialities like talking on girls, movies, apps, cars, wishes, etc. I find more important things to care about, like, in my country,*

> *little children beg in the streets. News doesn't show that. Child labor. Incompetent teachers. People killing people in the name of religions. Hatred. Racism. It all drives me mad."*

This young man's heart was broken, as was mine at the thought of losing him. My response said, in part, "The world desperately needs your insight and compassion. I share your sadness regarding the world as it is. For it to become what it must be, we need young people like you. If I can, in a small way, encourage you, and you live to make the world a bit brighter, my life will have meant more."

Since we first spoke, this young man has graduated from university and has a teaching position, family, and new home. I returned to Messenger to ask what his suffering taught him about affirming life. In part he replied:

> *"At University, I would get children from the street and feed them with what money I had and would be happy even when I went hungry myself. Today, if my students are suffering, I am always approachable. I try to help because I don't want my students to suffer what I suffered. What we need is a few words of kindness in this hectic life, to make someone's day, or to save a life."*

When a young Pakistani can bring tears to the eyes of an aging American across generations, cultures, and thousands of miles, it truly is a small world. And I am grateful beyond measure.

When I speak to groups, I will often ask, "How many of you have ever beat yourselves up in ways you know are unfair?" or "How many have said things to yourselves that you would *never* say to another human being?" Nearly every hand goes up, showing people tend to be harder on themselves than they deserve to be.

Those who know us and love us can see how we show up in the world and hold up a mirror to help us see. If they are genuinely loving, the mirror they hold up will be honest, raw, and unvarnished. Often, it will help us see a human with more kindness, sagacity, and love than what we see in ourselves. And when that voice of denial screams in our heads that they really do not know, or that they are just being polite, it is time to stop and realize they do know, and they are not lying. Then, it is time to find the courage to quiet that voice of denial and believe them.

One of the greatest gifts of being human, and one of the kindest, most generous things we can do for those we love, is to hold up a mirror and help them discover their beauty and magnificence. One of the kindest, most generous things we can do for ourselves is to find the courage to believe the people who love us when they hold up a mirror to help us see our own beauty and magnificence.

Chapter 7
What's Love Got to Do with It?

"Being deeply loved by someone gives you strength, while loving someone deeply gives you courage."

Lao Tzu

The man who called felt himself an abject failure. He had been out of work for months. After a frantic and challenging search, he did find a position, but it paid half that of his previous job. "I have failed my family. I am embarrassed and depressed. I love my wife and sons so much, and now I cannot even provide them with the life they deserve. I won't be able to send my sons to college or give my wife the comforts her friends enjoy. How could I have fallen so far?" He was in incredible pain over what he perceived to be his failures. He even began to feel his family might be better-off without him.

"Would you be willing to tell me about your wife and sons?" I asked. "I am the luckiest man in the world," he responded without hesitation. "I love my boys so much. They are amazing. They do well in school, they are athletes, and they have so many great friends. I have a wonderful relationship with each of them. They are a blessing!" "And your wife?" I pressed. "What can I say. She works incredibly hard. She cares for the three of us as if we were the only people on Earth. If it were not for her income these last few months, I do not know what we would have done. I won the lottery when I found her," he admitted. "It sounds as if you love them deeply," I responded. "More than you can imagine." So, I asked, "Do they love you?" After a short pause, he said, "I think so. My wife tells me all the time she does. With my boys, just knowing the great relationship we have, yeah, I am confident they love me."

"Could we return to the beginning of our conversation and talk about what you can and cannot provide your family?" I continued. "Sure," he said a bit quizzically. So, I asked, "Do you think any of them would give up, even for a second, your love, care and support, for more money?" After a pause, he admitted quietly, "No, probably not." "So, while you may not be able, at least for now, to provide monetary comfort, you give them wealth no amount of money could ever buy. Am I right?" I inquired. "When you put it that way, I guess you have a point," he admitted. "Could it be enough, at least for now, that you provide, not physical comfort, but great wealth through your love and support?" "Putting it that way, yeah I guess that could be enough for now," he said with growing confidence and renewed self-esteem. As we ended the call, I asked, "Would you give them each a hug tonight and tell them how much you love them and appreciate them." "I surely will. Thank you."

< >

One Christmas afternoon, I received an amazing gift. I answered a call from a young man in middle school. Through tears, he told me how he and his father argued constantly. "Because we argue so much, I wonder if my father actually loves me," he admitted. It would have broken my heart any afternoon but hearing this young man's doubts about his father's love on Christmas afternoon, brought me to tears.

The phone was not busy that afternoon, so I took considerable time to talk with this lost soul about the many ways he could approach his father and talk about their relationship. We spoke at length about how he might perceive his father's love even amidst the frequent harsh words they shared. When he shared that his father was under a great deal of stress at work, I asked if he might try to understand their relationship from his father's perspective. The longer we talked, the more ideas he thought of and the more his confidence grew. One of the last things he said before the call ended was "I know I don't know you well, but I love you." I fell in love with you too that afternoon, young man. Merry Christmas.

< >

One Snowball weekend, I got to know a young man I never expected would open up about his life. From the early moments on Friday morning, he demurred from hugging and maintained a friendly, but macho, distant aura. Even in our small group discussions, in which each of the other participants showed some level of vulnerability, he was kind and friendly, but aloof.

That ended late Saturday afternoon.

I do not recall the context of our conversation, but in one surprising moment this young man looked at us and exclaimed, "My father is my hero." Unexpectedly, he discovered his vulnerability and his macho mask vanished. "My dad is amazing. As a young man, he went through hell, including drug addictions and dealing. What amazes me is the way he got clean and works endlessly to provide for us. He is truly my hero." In the ensuing moments, his tears flowed freely, and the rest of us fell in love with this newly revealed facet of his being. "Have you ever told him what you just told us?" I asked. "I've tried," he said, "but it is hard. When I leave for school in the morning, I always say 'I love you,' as I walk out the door." "No," I pressed. "Have you ever looked him right in the eye and said

'Dad, you are my hero and I love you for all you have accomplished.'" "No," he admitted. "That would be really hard."

Just before the weekend ended, I caught up with this young man one last time. "One of the greatest gifts I ever received happened one Snowball weekend. My daughter looked me in the eye Sunday afternoon, as the weekend drew to a close, and told me something about her view of me that I will take with me to my grave. If you find the courage to tell your father what you told us, don't be surprised if he gets embarrassed and denies his significance. But know, he too, will take your words to his grave." "I'll try," he said. Then he gave me a hug.

Snowball retreats also offered tragic lessons on the human need for love. Far too often, the Saturday evening "It's a Wonderful Life" panel would include a teen, typically a young woman, who would tell us of an abusive relationship they escaped. They would describe young men who would belittle them, control them, typically demand sex, and have them believe they were responsible for the horrible treatment. Despite the pain these relationships caused, the teens, when asked why they stayed so long in a partnership that made them feel invisible, would reply, "I thought he cared. I believed his abuse was what love looked like." Those stories were so exceedingly difficult to hear. The only redeeming factor was that the teens eventually found the courage to care for themselves enough to cleanse the toxicity from their life.

One caller to the Lifeline told me her husband died six months earlier. After he passed, she discovered he had been a heroin addict which he hid from her. She was struggling to separate the kind wonderful husband she loved from the addict who lied to her, the person she never knew. I asked if it might be possible that because he loved her so much, he might have hidden his addiction for fear of losing her. Could she, I asked, accept his wholeness—the kind, wonderful husband along with his disease of addiction. She decided she could. She was going to sit down that afternoon and write him a letter of forgiveness and love. She knew it would help her heal.

Another caller, a young woman, found herself in a dreadful marriage. She had two children and, because she loved them so much, she knew she had to leave to protect them but was frightened. "I have no support. I have no idea how I could ever leave," she said with fear and trepidation in her voice. When she told me she had wonderful supportive parents who loved her a great deal, I asked if they knew the pain she was feeling. "Absolutely not! They think I have a perfect marriage. If I told them, it would cause them unbelievable pain. They would be on the first plane here and that would cause carnage in both families. I could never tell them." "Someday," I proceeded, "when your children are your age, if they find themselves in a frightening and painful place, will you want to know?" When she realized her parents' love for her was as deep as her love for her own children, she told me she would call her parents that very evening.

I had the privilege to speak with a young man suffering from numerous reversals in his life. He lost his job and was sinking into alcoholism. A relationship that meant a great deal to him ended. Tearfully, he described how frightened and alone he felt. "I cry a lot these days," he admitted. Even though his family lived on the other side of the country, I asked if he might gain support and comfort from his father and older brother. "You don't understand," he said with a hint of anger in his voice. "In my family, a man who admits to struggling is ridiculed. In their eyes, real men just suck it up. If I told them

I cried a lot, they would just laugh." How, I wondered, do we find ourselves in a culture that will not allow half the population to cry when their pain is overwhelming?

So, I asked, "What might happen if, the next time your brother ridicules you, you were to stop, look him in the eye and say 'Cut the crap. I am in real trouble and I need you. You are my brother, if you love me, I need you.'" He paused, and with a voice that clutched a bit of hope, said, "You know, that just might work."

What has love got to do with it? Everything.

Chapter 8
A Perfect Ending

"Perfect is the enemy of good."

Voltaire

Sometimes perfect finds us when we least expect it.

In the Fall of 2021, I was invited to give a keynote at a meeting of Chief Information Officers (CIOs) for school districts across the state of Illinois. I could never have conceived how this invitation would help save a life and change the future.

In March 2020, this group of professionals, and their staffs, navigated an enormous abyss as they, literally overnight, deployed relatively new and untested technology to reinvent the delivery of educational content as COVID-19 rendered traditional classroom technology obsolete. My task was to help them appreciate their success throughout 2020 and 2021. "It's true," I suggested, "educational outcomes were different from in-person teaching. However, if your people had not pivoted and put technology in every home, and found ways to support faculty, students, and parents, it is likely educational outcomes would have simply evaporated!"

In advance of my time with this incredible group of resolute professionals, I interviewed several of them to try to understand the enormity of the task handed to them as school doors slammed shut. The heroic stories I heard of the countless efforts put forth by their staffs were inspiring. These CIOs explained how boundaries disappeared. "I had to remind my people to put their phones away. 'Stop reading texts and emails for at least a few hours each day!' Some would have worked 24/7 had I not put a stop to it," one CIO told me.

But it was one call that changed the future. That CIO said, "My people strive for perfection. I remind them that perfect is the enemy of good. In these times, as painful as it might be, we must often settle for a good solution, because our customers are desperate." I was touched by that thought, not realizing how powerful Voltaire would become days later.

"My children are with relatives," she explained when I answered her call on the National Suicide Prevention Lifeline the following Saturday morning. "With them out of the house, it would be a good time for me to end my life." My heart broke for this young mother who believed she could not be the perfect mother her children deserved. To her that meant they would be better off without her. You see, her own parents were, suffice to say, unbelievably far from perfect. Her life was so painful, she wanted her children to have a life the opposite of the one she endured. She loved her children so much that nothing less than a perfect mother would suffice.

The turning point came when I reminded her of Voltaire's wisdom. She paused. "Could you say that again?" "When only perfection is acceptable," I said," you are blind to the loving parent you are; the truly good mother your children have." "Tell me one more time?" she asked. "Perfect is the enemy of good," I repeated. She began to cry, and through tears she said, "I'm going to write that down and carry it with me the rest of my life." Moments later that call ended with gratitude and tears on both ends of the line.

Two weeks later, in front of more than 80 school district CIOs, I was able to remind them of their value to the children, and future, of Illinois, and I was able to publicly thank one who helped me find a moment of perfection…a moment when the two of us were able to help a young mother find the courage to accept her imperfections, and know that being a good and loving mother was enough.

Months into the COVID-19 epidemic another young mother called. She was overwhelmed and in tears. She, too, aimed for perfection. She took immense pride in working full-time and keeping her home neat and orderly. Prior to COVID-19, albeit a challenge, she was able to keep up with cooking, cleaning, laundry and still have time to be the mother her children deserved, and the wife her husband loved. Then, the pandemic made her life immeasurably more complex. "In addition to everything else, suddenly I must help them with their schoolwork, watch over them as they struggle to learn remotely, and become an expert in remote technology I never knew existed. I cannot do it all. I feel such a failure."

"Of all the things you feel you should be doing, but cannot, what hurts the most?" I asked. With a pause she began to cry and said, "I can no longer be the mother my children need. They need the times we used to spend in the park…the times we would sit and read…the games we used to play." I thought for a moment and asked, "Could it be okay, just for now, that there are dirty clothes in the laundry room and dirty dishes in the sink so you could spend time with your children? Could you give up the need to be perfect in every way so you could spend time being the mother your children need?" The relief in her voice was palpable. As the call was ending, she said, "I am going to take the children to the park right now. Thank you so much."

I spoke with a preacher who was also a perfectionist. He hated himself because of all the ways he saw himself as imperfect. He put on a façade of perfection and refused to tell his congregation he was struggling. "They won't respect me if I am not perfect," he told me. He even admitted that his perfectionism and unhappiness led to anger and unhealthy treatment of his wife and four children. I asked if he ever told the members of his congregation that they deserve to love themselves unconditionally. "Of course! I do, all the time," he replied. "Do you see any hypocrisy in not, at least trying, to love yourself in spite of your failings?" I asked. "When you put it that way, I do. But loving myself despite my failings is exceedingly difficult," he admitted. "What might happen," I continued, "if you were to reflect on that?" I suggested he even consider writing a sermon in which he admitted to his congregation how he, too, struggles with self-acceptance. "How do you think they would feel if you were to tell them you will be working to love yourself, and ask for their support and prayers during your journey?" He admitted that doing that would lift the great weight of perfection off his shoulders.

Often, I am asked how I dealt with the stress of answering calls on the suicide hotline. There were two things that helped. First, the emotion that typically overwhelmed me as I closed the door after a 4-hour shift, was gratitude. How I could not be grateful when a young mother came to realize the love for her children, in the end, was infinitely more important than her need for perfection. Or when a young teen called holding a bottle of pills she intended to ingest, ended our call 45 minutes later by thanking me for answering. "If you hadn't, I would have taken those pills."

The second way I tried not to let the intensity of the work overwhelm me, was giving myself permission to be imperfect. I am, after all, simply a member of the community who showed up one afternoon each week to help in whatever way I could. I may have failed to help every caller find their perfect ending, but I always tried.

Chapter 9
When Culture Intercedes

Luis, a wonderful young man in Operation Snowball, lost his younger brother to suicide as a sophomore in high school. As you might imagine, his entire family was devastated.

As they planned a celebration of the young man's life, Luis asked me to speak to the family and friends who would be present that Sunday afternoon. I was honored…and terrified. Luis and his brother were first generation in this country; their parents having immigrated from Mexico. The audience would be friends and neighbors who grew up in Mexico, in a culture for which I had little to no understanding. They braved hardships beyond anything I could imagine stitching together a life for themselves and their children. They had nothing when they arrived and have immense pride in having made a life in a new and foreign land.

I felt unprepared, vulnerable, and naked in my ignorance. How could I speak of something so intimate as the loss of a child, with a hundred or more people whose life, culture, values, and life experiences were so different from mine? I spoke to Luis of my fears and trepidation, but he insisted. He was hopeful my experiences on the suicide hotline might reach across any divide and help save the lives of other young Hispanic youth who might be at risk. It was impossible to say no to a young man who loved me so very much.

Because I knew Luis' friends and teachers, most of whom understood what it meant to grow up Hispanic in America, I spent hours trying to discern words I might summon that would have meaning, even in some modest way.

Two messages became clear. First, parents who struggled to give their children a good life felt their children had no right to feel troubled. Secondly, their children were forbidden to speak of their troubles with anyone outside the family.

Here, then, is what I shared.

> *Thank you for this opportunity to be with you today. I am here because a mother and father lost their child to suicide. I wish that tragedy never occurred, but it did. My hope is to use this occasion to prevent this from happening to any more children.*
>
> *I am also here because I have been a volunteer on a suicide hotline for many years and have talked with thousands of human beings in pain. I have talked with children, teens, adults, and seniors, many of whom have contemplated ending their lives.*
>
> *I am here because of a wonderful organization known as Operation Snowball, which helps teens lead healthy lives and deal with the challenges of becoming an adult in an increasingly difficult world. It is through Operation Snowball that many teens, including many of your children, have allowed me to love them, and they have loved me in return.*
>
> *Across America, and the world, we are facing an epidemic of suicide among teens. No one knows why, but if my being here can help prevent even one, it will have been a tremendous victory.*
>
> *If there is one thing I hope you will remember from today it is this: you matter in the lives of your children. They need to know they are important and loved by you. They want to know they matter in your eyes. If you are like me, it is easy to believe we don't matter to our children. It is so easy to feel we are a failure in their eyes—that we are not deserving of their love and respect—but nothing is farther*

from the truth. They truly want to love you...and they desperately want your love in return.

I know you grew up in a difficult, often frightening world. Most of you have faced and overcome difficulties I cannot even imagine. I stand here inspired by your courage and strength.

While you may believe your children live a life made easy by your sacrifices, they are becoming adults in a world made horribly difficult in many other ways.

Today, teens face insults and cruelty, not only at school, but every moment of every day through the Internet and social media. We live in a world of prejudice and hate against people of color. Your children face that every single day.

The economy makes it difficult for any of us to know with certainty that we will be able to support our families. Imagine how frightening this can be for a teen who may not even be able to find a summer job, let alone a career to support a family.

Terrorism highlights our daily news, cancer seems to impact every family and neighborhood, war rages in many parts of the world.

In the face of bullying, an uncertain economy, and horrific world news, how does it feel when a young personal world seems to fall apart—a parent yells, a clique becomes brutal, a failing grade appears, an important friendship ends? Do we really know?

It is easy to think our lives were difficult and that our children have been given so very much; they have no reason for sadness, depression, or suicide. But the things we have been given, the lives that have been handed to us, are meaningless if we are frightened, scared, or feel hopeless. If we do not have people in our lives who can listen, truly listen, look us in the eye, and tell us we are okay, life can be overwhelming.

If you demand your children speak only to you; if you prevent them from speaking to others about the challenges they face, you prevent them from learning how to face fears that even we cannot understand. As parents, we need ears that can hear…not those of judgment. Ears that hear their fear and know it is real. Ears that will not compare their lives to ours, and dismiss their fear, but will hear that their lives are different than ours and can be frightening despite our belief it is not.

And if your children find another person in whom to confide, another who will listen in a way that we, as parents, cannot, then, rather than seeing it as an insult to the family, rejoice that your child has found someone to save them. One of the saddest moments I face with teens is when I learn of an aunt, uncle, cousin, teacher, or minister in whom they would love to confide but cannot. My heart breaks when they tell me, "If my, parents ever found out, they would never forgive me!"

If you see signs in your children that worry you. If they withdraw…if their habits change unexpectedly…if the patterns of their lives alter in startling ways…it is time to seek help. And it is okay to admit you don't know what to do. There are resources to help. Talk with a trusted relative, minister, priest, school counselor, the wonderful adults in Operation Snowball. Call the National Suicide Prevention Lifeline. Please do something. Because if you choose to simply tell your children to get on with life because you have given them all they need, then you are withholding the one thing they need more than anything…your understanding.

So, I have a final word for you. It is a single word. Love. Love them for who they are. Love them even though you do not understand them. Love them even though they are unable to understand you. But don't just tell them you love them. Actions speak louder than words; show them you love them. Tell them you love them in every way you possibly can.

It has been said that youth are the messages we send to a world we will never see. Let us, at this very moment, commit to sending them into that world knowing they are loved.

Gracias.

Chapter 10
The Power of Vulnerability

"It must have been a place so dark you couldn't feel the light, reaching for you through that stormy cloud."

Country Music Group Rascal Flatts

Years ago, two high school students chose to end their lives a few months apart. They were close friends, and, as a result, their parents were thrust into a world of pain and unimaginable loss.

In the years since the loss of those two young people, I have agonized over our collective inability to put our arms around them and help them feel the light—and love—reaching for them through the stormy clouds that defined the tragic moments in their lives.

As I reflected on our failure, I was reminded of words from William Bridges, author of the book *Transitions.* "One thing kids need is honesty. They need a realistic picture of what it is like to be an adult—that you are confused so much of the time and frequently really scared. I hear parents talking about setting a good example for their children. Their version means never saying any of that stuff. So, we are producing kids who do not know what to make of fear and confusion when they encounter it."

Recall from Chapter 2, the elder who considered suicide in his younger years, wrote a great deal about it, but had not shared those stories with his children and grandchildren. The courage and vulnerability it takes to share the most painful and intimate moments of our lives are immense. However, by modeling those critical values, we give future generations permission to experience the challenges they face and speak of them with equal courage and vulnerability. We model for them the ways we have found to feel light that reaches for us through the stormy clouds. Only after we show them our vulnerability, have we earned the right to put our arms around them and help them reach for the light on the other side of their own darkness.

When a grandfather loses a grandson to suicide with no indication it was eminent, is there another way? Was the child aware his grandfather also suffered through bouts of fear and confusion, as he surely did in his lifetime? Were there windows of opportunity to model vulnerability that remained shuttered?

In addition to sharing our fear and confusion, I wonder if living in a more honest world means listening more intensely to our children about how complex and frightening this world must seem. I grew up during the emerging cold war, the proliferation of bomb shelters and school drills to protect us from a nuclear attack. It was scary. But today, terrorism and violence highlight our daily news, global warming is a growing threat, environmental disasters blare for weeks, the cancer epidemic impacts every family and neighborhood, war rages, or threatens to erupt, around the globe. Shall I continue? And, because of instant, global communication, the threats do not hesitate for an instant to insert themselves into our lives.

In the face of such an onslaught, how might it feel when a young, personal world begins to crumble?

Twice each year, as I contemplated our Operation Snowball weekends, I wondered about the appropriate role for me, as an adult, with the teens. Whenever I recall Neil Postman's thought that youth are messages we send to a future we will not see, my heart breaks. I know that someday, in the natural course of events, I will no longer be here for my children in their time of need, nor for other young people who need a kind word or hug to help them understand that, despite their pain, they will be okay.

But I wonder if my heartache comes from a deeper place. I wonder if the tears might emanate from a deep sense of inadequacy. Who am I to think I am wise enough to teach these young people even a modest portion of what they need to know as they navigate the treacherous rapids hurling us into the future. Who am I to think I can pass along a single skill they will require to live into the future, and, along the way, find fulfillment and a share of happiness? Who am I to think I have the capacity to give them the love they ache to find in their lives?

The reality is that these are the wrong questions. These questions put me at the center of their future. These questions hold out the possibility that I have their answers, when, in fact, I cannot even answer the deepest questions in my own life.

So, what might be better questions? Here are a few that come to mind.

How can I model for these ambassadors to the future the search for self?

How can I, by honestly revealing the hills and valleys—the oft frightening stormy clouds—of my own path, help them know the path they are on is the right path, even though, for so many, their path is infinitely more difficult than mine?

How can I learn to find and bow to the sacredness inside myself, and by so doing, point the way to their learning of their own wholeness?

How can I learn that the answers I seek about life in general, and my life in particular, are here inside my heart and that if I trust, they will reveal themselves?

How can I help others discover they already have the answers they seek?

So now, my closing thoughts reflect the enormous gratitude I owe the thousands of teens I have come to know.

> *Thank you for courageously sharing moments when it was impossible to see the light reaching through the often-stormy clouds that drift through your life. Thank you for hearing me when I look into your eyes and affirm your beauty and significance.*
>
> *Through your courage, authenticity, and vulnerability, you have gifted me with the most stunning and joyful moments any human could imagine. You have shown me how the tears born of pain can become the tears of joy in a moment of sharing. I now understand how the magnificent beauty of life cannot be separated from its darker moments.*
>
> *Life is difficult, however, if that is all you allow yourself to see, you discount the extraordinary complexity that makes this world so remarkable. Each of us is unique; each lives a life never lived by another human being. Each is given a glimpse of what it means to be human that has never been seen and will never be seen again. Through your experience of pain and sorrow, life is granting you the wisdom to look into the eyes of another and say, "I understand something of what life is trying to teach. Allow me to help you find the path forward and see other ways."*
>
> *Whether you can see it or not, the world desperately needs the insight life is trying to share through you. If you will summon the courage to embrace pain, be vulnerable, and share its ensuing wisdom, the Universe has infinite joy and beauty it is willing to share.*

So, I bow to each of you. I bow to your goodness…I bow to your humanity…I bow to your wisdom. And I ask for your love and support as I try to bow to myself.

Chapter 11
Tough Love

There are, unfortunately, times during which the only way to help another person see a new way forward is by leaving them no alternative.

Near tears, he stood at my door one evening and pleaded, "Mr. Breisch, you have to let me out of my second-year French class."

During my four years teaching high school math, I lived in the school dormitory with freshmen and sophomores. Even though I was less than ten years their senior, I was responsible for the lives of forty or more young men. I was also faculty advisor to many.

Sean was one of the freshman residents and one of my advisees. Since he was in one of my Algebra I classes, I knew him to be a dedicated and disciplined young man. He was smart, hard-working, friendly, and always well-prepared. He was a joy to have in class.

However, standing in my doorway with his request was one of the most difficult moments of my brief tenure as a high school teacher. I wasn't even sure the school administration would allow me to demand his placement be changed. Nonetheless, I was determined to help Sean witness the abilities I could see in him; abilities that eluded him in that moment.

I could tell by the look in his eyes that he was terrified. "I have been placed in Mrs. Beauchene's second year French class and I'm going to fail!" He had been in French I with a teacher whose demands on his students were, shall we say, modest. Mrs. Beauchene, on the other hand, was known to be a highly effective instructor with high expectations of her students.

Since I had not been in either classroom, I had no way to know how difficult the transition would be for Sean. However, I had great faith in his ability and was confident he could scale the cliff ahead.

I looked him in the eye and said, "I'm sorry, Sean. I will not let you out of Mrs. B's class. I know you. I know of your abilities and your work ethic. I am certain you can handle this challenge."

He continued to plead with me, but, I was unwilling to change my mind. He returned to his room in tears. I closed the door to my apartment, confident of my decision, but heartbroken. You cannot help but wonder in those moments, if you have truly made the correct decision.

I need not have worried. Sean, as I suspected, excelled under the tutelage of Mrs. B. After every test, Sean would show up in my classroom, or at the door to my apartment and share his success.

I have had, over the years, many friends and acquaintances, who had to deal with loved ones whose pleas for leniency were far more difficult to deny than what I faced with Sean. It is heartbreaking to watch a friend having to decide between loving acceptance of destructive behavior or tough love. When you truly love someone, the hope that loving acceptance will win out is strong. The thought of throwing down the gauntlet, and demanding new behavior, can be terrifying. I have never been faced with such an excruciating decision regarding someone I care deeply about. If I do, I pray for the courage to do the best I can and hope the one I love loves themselves enough to find their own salvation. As I always said about callers to the suicide hotline, it was never my role to save them. They and they alone could save themselves, or not.

Chapter 12
The Gift of New Eyes

A young woman called suffering from a disease that severely limited the things she could do and would, eventually, cut her life extremely short. Her mother constantly lamented the myriad experiences her daughter would never enjoy—everything from a glass of wine to having children. Every visit home, faced with an onslaught of lamentations, the caller told me how she struggles to find words that would enable her mother to witness the wholeness of her life rather than its perceived brokenness. "I sometimes dread going home knowing that as soon as I walk through the door, my mother will not see me. She will only see my brokenness."

We talked for a long time as I tried to put myself in her shoes and understand her challenging life. She explained that, while she sometimes finds the disease difficult, she has a deep appreciation for the life that results from it. "Since I cannot party like so many of my friends, I have come to appreciate and enjoy the solitude it has given me. I love the time I have to myself and have found it easy to pore myself in my studies." After listening to her experiences and wisdom, I expressed my appreciation. "As much as I would love to take away the challenges you face, what I hear is that, in very real ways, this disease has been a gift in your life. You have experienced things that gave your life more meaning."

As she pondered that thought, she suddenly paused and said, "I know what I am going to say to my mother the next time she begins to lament my life. I am going to look her in the eyes and say, 'Mom, what you refuse to see is all you have missed by not having this illness!'"

It was a stunning moment. I felt as though this woman had given me new eyes. My old eyes, when in the presence of a person who may lack abilities, were blinded by assumptions of what they were missing in their lives. The eyes she gifted me, by surrendering those assumptions, began to see worlds that were always there, but to which I was blind—Universes in which others are not lacking in abilities; they are given capabilities, capacities, and wisdom I would never have.

< >

My years volunteering on the suicide hotline gave me many treasures, but few were greater than the those I received from a fellow volunteer. Kim's wisdom as a counselor was unequaled, and her capacity to teach new trainees gifted them with essential skills; competencies that helped them immeasurably when facing another's difficult life circumstances.

However, it was the way Kim approached life itself from which I learned the greatest lessons. You see, Kim became blind at a young age. Having Kim as a friend brought astonishing meaning to the phrase "The gift of new eyes."

Kim's generosity and concern for others was inspiring. One afternoon, she and I attended a monthly training session. That afternoon her husband was unable to pick her up, so she asked if I might give her a ride home. I was delighted, not only to help, but also to gain additional insight from her about the topic we had been discussing. However, during the entire ride, I worried what I should do when we arrived in her driveway. Part of me wanted to be a gentleman and offer to help her reach her front door. But another voice screamed its dissent. "How dare you treat this woman as if she were incapable of taking care of herself. How could you insult her that way?"

When we finally arrived, the first impulse took over, and I asked if she would like me to help her to her front door. "If it would make you feel better, that would be fine," she told me. Kim, never one to focus on herself, strove to help me in my time of need.

Kim never missed anything in her life. She accomplished everything others would—more than most—including traveling the world with her husband. Kim's other senses made up for her lack of eyesight. She would recognize a person entering a room the moment the first syllables escaped their lips. I suspect, if anyone ever spoke about the things she missed in her life, she would have thought, "What you refuse to see is all you have missed because you can see!"

In "An Immense World," by Ed Yong, I discovered the many ways in which I, too, am disabled in comparison with millions of other species. A dog, with its exceptional sense of smell, can detect a single fingerprint after a week on an exposed rooftop. Bees, which taste with their feet, will detect the sweetness of nectar just by standing on a flower. There are species that can see ultraviolet light. Elephants can listen across distances through the vibrations they feel on their feet. Whales can be heard as far away as 10,000 miles and map the ocean floor using echolocation. Similarly, bats use echolocation to recognize the shape and texture of their world. Octopus' eight arms, and hundreds of suckers, taste, explore, and understand the world through multiple independent brains. Eagles have eyes that can observe a rodent half a mile away.

Humans have a marvelous combination of senses that enable us to navigate the world we know. But, if you study the capabilities of millions of other species, it turns out the world we know is the thinnest sliver of what exists.

By peering through the eyes, hearts, and souls, of other humans and other species, I experience wisdom, beauty, and elegance in a Universe in which it is I who is less-than-able in countless and profound ways. In such a world, the word "disabled" ceases to have meaning, and "other-abled" is a term I have added to my personal vocabulary.

Chapter 13
Changing the World is an Inside Job

He sat alone in the corner of the room with his head buried in his hands. When one of the other adults on the Snowball weekend suggested he might need a hug, I offered to speak with him. As I approached, he looked up and I asked if he was okay. With sad, averted eyes he told me he was.

As I turned to leave, something inside begged me not to walk away; I knew he was not speaking the truth of his life. I returned, looked into his eyes, and said, "I heard your words, but this is what your body language said, 'I am really not okay, but you are not the person I would talk with about it.' You do not need to talk with me; I just want to know you have someone with whom you can talk." In that instant, his body language changed, and our relationship took a remarkable turn. He stood up, looked directly into my eyes, and said, "Thank you, I am going through some tough times, but I'll be okay…and yes, I do have people I can talk with." I offered him a hug and left. I still did not even know his name.

At the end of the weekend, intermixed with numerous "warm fuzzies" [5] written by participants, was one that said, in part, "You've shown that some people really do care. You've given me a reason to carry on." The note was signed, "Love, Dakota." Several days later I confirmed that this kind and

---

[5] All through the 3-day Snowball weekends, whenever we found a few precious moments, we would write notes of affirmation—we called them "warm fuzzies"—to participants who helped make our weekend remarkable. It was so important for several of the adults to communicate our love for these remarkable young people. Despite getting to bed after midnight, we'd rise at 4am to gather in the dining room to commune, enjoy each other's company, and write until our hands cramped! It was such a great joy.

generous note was from the young man with whom I had the brief exchange the Saturday before.

For the next two years, I saw Dakota on Snowball weekends and at occasional Thursday night meetings. We shared emotionally horrible times, including the suicide of his father. Dakota continued to affirm—through sincere embraces and kind, generous words—the beautiful person he saw in me, even if I was unable to see it in myself. I too, spoke to him of the beautiful young man he had become—a person able to instantly see, and speak to, the beauty in others.

After he graduated from high school, our opportunity to see, or speak with, one another became increasingly rare. A graduation gift, and text and voice messages, went unanswered.

The year ended quietly in my life, but I awoke early New Year's morning to learn that the young man who so often pointed to my inner beauty had taken his life in the moments before the new year arrived. As hard as so many of us tried, Dakota was never able to see the gifts we could see shining from within him.

On the first anniversary of his suicide, I sat with tears welling up…tears that represented a mix of sadness over losing him, and guilt for not being there one more time to draw him back into his life…a life that touched and changed many others.

As each new year unfolds, I resolve yet again, to help others see the beauty that exists within them. But I remain cognizant that the only one who I can truly help see inner beauty in is me. If I cannot learn to witness mine, I remain a hypocrite when I try to point others towards theirs. Changing the world truly is an inside job.

I still love you, Dakota. I miss you terribly. And I am forever grateful that you remain one of my most profound teachers.

Chapter 14
Surrender...It's not for the Faint of Heart

"Try to get over the narrow idea that surrender is abject defeat. Surrender, in spirituality, is total acceptance."

From the Bhagavad Gita, as translated by Jack Hawley

When he finished playing, we embraced, and I told him how he and his music have taught me a great deal about life.

Jeff filled our house with music many times in the years since he and my daughter became friends. Typically, night has overtaken us as he lowers himself onto the piano bench. He asks if it is okay to turn down the lights; he prefers to play in near darkness. Within moments, Jeff, the instrument, and the music become one. I wonder if he places his fingers on the keyboard, or if the keys reach upward to find them. In those moments, music, piano, and musician relinquish individual identities and surrender to what is called from them collectively. Jeff's hands and fingers move effortlessly, called into position by the music and the instrument that will declare it to the world. The experience brings tears to my eyes.

I have a sense that if Jeff tried to rein in the music and piano, forcing them to do his bidding—failing to accept the latent invitation into the communal creation—the room would become infused with notes borne of conflict and control, rather than music that emanates from generosity, love, and relationship.

We live in a world that would have me believe, with enough effort—more force and control—I can fill the future with music of my own making. I can rein in the world and make it do my bidding. Should I fail to align the world with my vision, it is solely due to a lack of effort and diligence. Jeff, the music, and the piano invite me to see the world in a new way: divine my path through surrender rather than diligence. In this world, I relinquish my individuality, accept the invitation to be found, and give of myself without reservation. When I find the courage required by surrender, the future arises from generosity, love, and relationship…and is infinitely more beautiful than anything I could even imagine on my own.

The world of surrender, for me, is a brave new world…a truly foreign, oft frightening, land. But in a book I read recently, the author suggested, in those moments when life offers comfort or fear, we should choose fear. Comfort confirms what we already know. Fear offers the possibility of learning and wisdom. My real life exists in that brave new world, so here is to surrender, fear and courage.

Thank you, Jeff, for this exquisite lesson.

Chapter 15
Guilt, The Hidden Mental Illness

After we connected, he explained he left work early. “I'm in my car on the way to the emergency room and just needed someone to talk to.”

“I am glad you called. What is making life so difficult?” I asked. “I have been diagnosed with bipolar disorder and anxiety. I was at my desk this afternoon when I suddenly found myself formulating a plan to end my life. I attempted suicide a couple of years ago and did not want to go there again. When I felt myself slipping back into that awful, awful place, I knew I needed to do something. So, I am on my way to the emergency room.”

During our dialogue, he mentioned he lived at home with his parents, so I asked, “Do they know about your past attempt and how you're feeling his afternoon?” “When I attempted, they were very understanding and supportive. But it was so difficult, I simply cannot put them through that again,” he replied. “Even if I wanted to tell them, I have waited too long. I should have reached out days ago when I first felt myself slipping. I let them down again. So now I feel the need to handle this on my own.”

“So,” I suggested, “on top of your depression, anxiety, and suicidal ideation, you are burdening yourself with guilt for what your family went through in the past, and because of that you have not reached out to them this time. Is that right?” “Yes,” he admitted, “I feel horrible. They do not deserve any of this.”

I asked if he thought he could separate his guilt from his depression, anxiety, and ideation. When he said he thought he could, I asked, “If you let the guilt evaporate, even for a moment, how do you feel?" He paused and said it felt like a great weight suddenly lifted.

With mental illness, as opposed to a disease like cancer, the messages we receive imply it is our fault. We are simply not strong enough. "Just smile more." "You have no right to feel so sad." "Look at all the gifts in your life." "So many have it much worse than you." The guilt we layer on our already overwhelmed sense of self, is the oft-hidden monster we should not have to slay.

"If you opened up with your parents this afternoon about your current feelings, do you think some of your guilt might actually evaporate?" I asked. He admitted that if he could be honest with his parents, he would feel a great deal better. I suggested he could choose one of two courses of action: continue to the emergency room or go home and talk with his parents. "Either is an appropriate way to care for yourself, but which choice feels right in *this* moment?" Without pausing he told me that he wanted to talk with his father. "I can always go to the emergency room after we talk if the two of us feel it's best."

Just before we ended the call, he said, "Thank you so much!" I said, "No, thank you. Thank you for finding the self-love and courage to decide you were worth saving."

< >

Recall the young man in the Introduction, who asked "Do you think the pain I am feeling is my heart trying to find its way back into the world?" That young man called because of his certainty he made his young family's life exceedingly difficult. "Months ago, I was offered an opportunity that would have provided my family with many resources. It would have made my wife's life much easier and provided a better future for our children. I made a poor decision when I turned it down. How could I have been so stupid?" he asked. The guilt he felt was relentless. I asked if he would take me back to the moments before he rejected the opportunity. "It would have been a big promotion and tremendous responsibility," he explained. There was a tone in his voice that led me to ask, "Were you frightened?" "I was. I was terrified I would not be successful and felt I might fail," he admitted. So, I proceeded, "Let's walk back to the moment you said 'No.' In that moment did you do the best you could? I understand, in retrospect, the decision appears quite different, but in *that* moment, did you do the best you could, knowing what you knew then?" He paused and then quietly admitted he really felt he did.

Once he realized he may have done the best he could, and the guilt eased, he began to reflect on the heartache he still felt. It was in that reflective moment that he asked if I thought his heart was trying to find its way back into the world. The sagacity that emerged from callers, especially those years younger than I, filled me with humility. Years later, I still reflect on that extraordinary insight born from a moment's reprieve from relentless guilt.

Remorse is a valuable emotion. It helps me remember I am capable of more. I cannot do it all, but I can always do more. When I recall the hundreds of times I fail others…walk past humans living on the street…am unable to help millions who live in poverty while I have so much….am judgmental of others, in ignorance of their circumstances…when I remember the hundreds of times I was not the man, nor the father and husband, I wished to be—remorse is an appropriate response.

However, guilt can overwhelm. The crushing pain it provides, on top of the pain life provides, can bring us to our knees and make the journey into the future seem pointless. In those moments it can help to separate the guilt from the pain of life and recall it just might be helping your heart find its way back into the world.

Chapter 16
Pain, An Unlikely Source of Wisdom

"It's So Counterintuitive!" she said. "Yes, it is," I replied.

The young woman suffered from sporadic, chronic, gastrointestinal pain. She thought she might have eaten something the prior weekend that aggravated the condition, and, as a result, she was in great pain. I asked if she would be willing to take a moment to focus on the pain. "Truly feel it…try not to fear or avoid it," I asked. After a few moments I asked how she felt. She revealed there was considerably less pain. "It's interesting," she said. "A moment ago, I felt pain through my entire body. Now, as I experience it, and accept it rather than fight it, I realize it is centered in my abdomen. The pain throughout the rest of my body is gone.

She admitted that when I first suggested she stop trying to distract herself, and instead acknowledge and accept the pain, it felt counterintuitive. It is. The fear of pain causes us to conjure images of it eating us alive. We fear it will never cease. It can take us captive and refuse to let us escape its clutches. When we focus on pain, accept rather than fight it, we come to appreciate and acknowledge its true size, shape, and scope. The fear we have lessens, and its grasp on us loosens.

Near the end of the call, she asked if a similar practice might help with emotional pain. I said I have seen that as well.

Weeks later, I spoke with a young man, distraught because he feared an important relationship in his life might be ending. He was not sure he had the strength to deal with such tremendous loss; his girlfriend meant the world to him. In a similar fashion I asked this young man to focus on the sadness and fear and try to accept rather than deny them. We sat quietly. Then he began to speak. "What was so helpful in those moments was the insight I gained by exploring my feelings. I realized that a great deal of my fear comes from blaming myself for every failure in the relationship, from the smallest to the most egregious. I was able to separate the sadness over the loss from the life-deadening guilt of feeling I am not enough. While I do not want the relationship to end, I can admit that it may simply be due to incompatibility and not because I am inept or cruel. When I tell myself I am enough, I know, if this relationship does fail, I will find another that is even more fulfilling; she will too."

A teen called to talk about how her father's comments made her feel worthless. When I asked if she thought she was worthless, she told me she did not. "I have friends who tell me I am not. I guess, next time my father tells me I am worthless I am going to remember I am not," she admitted. Near the end of our call, she exhibited insight and wisdom I did not expect from someone her age. I asked how she would feel about these years when she was thirty. "I'm going to know they taught me strength," she said with renewed self-confidence.

I do not, even for a moment, wish to discount or downplay the physical and emotional pain suffered by the thousands of souls I spoke to over the years. A young woman in her twenties felt pain from head to toe from the moment she awoke to the moment she put head to pillow. A recent surgery meant to help, made it worse. I cannot imagine living with such a demon every waking moment, nor would I even know how to ask her to acknowledge and accept such anguish.

None of us wishes to live in pain, but, when we find ways to befriend it, accept it, and converse with it, it can, occasionally, offer insights that are profound and even lifesaving. The pain and heartache can indeed be an unlikely source of wisdom.

Chapter 17
Gifts Delivered with Courage

I learned a valuable, touching lesson from a man with aphasia; a condition that makes communication difficult and afflicts more than two million people in the United States.

For fifteen years, I wrote essays for a bi-monthly community magazine. Initially, I was invited to contribute because of my position as Executive Director of the local Chamber of Commerce. It seemed a great opportunity to promote the vibrancy of commerce throughout the community. I tried to do that, I really did, at least the first year. Then, my need to discuss what mattered to me overtook my fingers as they danced across my computer's keyboard.

Over the years, I received compliments on the thoughts, and the words that delivered them. One summer day as I walked the bike path next to a river that flows through town—reading a book as I strolled—a man came up from behind on his bicycle. "Are you Roger?" he asked. Whenever I get that question from a person I do not know, I can guess I have been recognized from my articles and the picture that accompanied them. "I was riding the other way when I recognized you," he told me. "I had to turn around to speak to you." He told me how he appreciated my essays, and that there was one he found particularly meaningful. "My son suffers from anxiety and depression," he explained. "It has been exceedingly difficult; heart-breaking because my wife and I do not know how to help. He is often angry because he does not understand why he has been singled out by these afflictions. You wrote a piece about encountering that on the suicide hotline, so I left a copy for my son in hopes he will read it and we can talk." Our paths comingled for another mile or so while we shared an extended, heart-warming conversation. After our paths diverged, I was overwhelmed with gratitude. If words given to me could open a life-affirming conversation between father and son, I am truly blessed.

But this is about aphasia, not anxiety and depression. There is a man at the gym I attend for whom walking is a challenge. I am always impressed by the determination he displays as he completes multiple laps around the track. One morning, as I was preparing to leave, I felt a tap on my shoulder, only to discover it was the gentleman whose determination I had been appreciating moments earlier. He paused; it was clear he was struggling to find a word. Then, he asked "Batavia?" I acknowledged that yes, I live in Batavia. He struggled again and said, "I'm sorry, I suffer from aphasia." I thanked him for helping me understand. It was clear he had something in mind when he said, "That…that…" I wondered if he recognized me from my articles, so I took a small risk and asked if he was thinking about the magazine and my articles. He smiled and said "Yes…magazine articles. Thank you. That is all," and turned to walk away.

It is a gift when anyone tells me of a positive relationship they have found with my words. However, this man must, every day, summon the courage required to meet a world that can be cruel in the face of human challenges. That morning, he found the courage to thank me for my words. Of all the kind and generous words used to describe my essays, it is the courage represented by these five, "Thank you. That is all," that still brings me to tears.

I have, many times, hesitated to say something to someone who I appreciate for fear that what I say will not be enough. This kind soul reminds me that it is always enough if the words are given with sincerity, kindness, and courage.

Sometimes, the Universe conspires to offer gifts that take astonishing courage to deliver. Recall the story of Dakota, the young man from Snowball who, after graduating from high school, chose to end his life. I attended his wake and funeral early the following week. I met his mother for the first time at his wake, attended by hundreds who knew and loved him. We waited in line for hours for a brief opportunity to offer words that might mean something amid crushing, overwhelming grief. When the moment arrived for me to face Dakota's mother, I introduced myself. Her eyes, already having shed a river of tears, filled one more time as she told me how much I meant to her son. I could no longer hold back my own tears. We parted with a heartfelt hug.

The following day, when Dakota's funeral ended, I headed for my car. As I left the church, I wished for one last opportunity to offer comfort to his mother. Certain she would be surrounded by family and friends, I hesitated to even attempt to find her. However, I turned around anyway and discovered, to my astonishment, she stood alone next to the hearse that held her son. It was an unexpected and unmistakable invitation to give her one more hug. As soon as she saw me, she became animated. "Roger," she began, "I am so confused, and frightened. All morning, I have been hearing Dakota say to me 'Talk to the children. Talk to the children.' I have no idea what that means. Dakota knew I am not religious and am unsure of the afterlife. I do not know what it means, or what to do with it, but I hear him over and over."

Dakota's cremation and internment were not scheduled until the following weekend, so I asked, "I don't know what Dakota could be asking of you, but we both know of his love for Snowball and the teens he met there. We meet every Thursday evening. It seems far too much to ask that you come and speak to the teens this Thursday, before you have even laid your son to rest, but would you consider speaking to the teens who grieve his loss?" "If you think it would be appropriate, I'd be willing to try," she told me.

Dakota's mother, unsure her words would find meaning in the hearts of the teens, spoke simply of him and the unbearable grief at his loss. She touched many lives that night and saved at least one. One teen, I will call her Susan, had been struggling with thoughts of suicide and had decided, earlier in the week, that, since she would be home alone that Thursday evening, it would be the perfect opportunity to end her life. A friend, a guardian angel, had called Susan that afternoon and pleaded with her to drive her to Snowball. This angel had no other way to get there, and she wanted to hear Dakota's mother. Susan protested but eventually acquiesced. After the meeting, Susan told us that it was Dakota's mother's compelling testimony that opened her eyes to the pain she would cause her family if she ended her life. Dakota's mother did speak to the children, through a voice only her pain and anguish could make evident to those teens.

The gifts we receive make our lives better and often fill us with joy. However, when those gifts require astounding courage on the part of the giver, I am incredibly thankful to have received them.

Chapter 18
Good Trouble

"I'm a burden to everybody," she began when I answered the Lifeline. "Everyone would be better off if I wasn't here." "Are you considering suicide?" I asked. She paused and quietly admitted she was. I asked her first name and age, for familiarity and a bit of context. "I'm Mary (not her real name) and I'm almost 14." It broke my heart that a person so young believes others would be better off if she ended her life.

I asked why she feels a burden to others. "I frequently get in trouble at school and it's really hard on my mother." When I asked for an example, she related the following: "We are reading *To Kill a Mockingbird* in class, and the author uses the 'N' word throughout the book. My teacher insisted that, given the time it was written, and to make the story real, it was necessary to use that word. That upset me. I raised my hand and asserted there should have been a way to write the story without the 'N' word. The teacher said I was wrong, sent me to the principal, and he called my mother."

"I can see merit in both sides," I replied, "but your teacher was unwilling to engage in a discussion?" "Yes. She just told me I was wrong."

"If I asked your mother, would she say you are a burden." "Probably not, but even if she doesn't say it, I wonder if she sometime thinks I am."

Since the example she gave me was over an issue she felt was important, I asked if she also gets into trouble for things that may be silly or trivial. She said that seldom happens. "Most often I get into trouble because of something I believe is wrong. When I have something to say, and speak up, even my friends roll their eyes. I make everyone's lives difficult."

"Would it be fair to suggest you are trying to make the world a better place?" I asked. When she admitted she did, a thought occurred to me. "I can't recall his name, but a black congressman passed away recently who did change the world." "Do you mean John Lewis?" she asked. I was stunned. "You're 13 and you know of John Lewis?" She said she did but did not know too much about him. I told her that one of his favored principles was "Make good trouble." I suggested she might be doing what John Lewis asked of each of us.

"People who change the world, often make those around them uncomfortable. It is impossible to nudge the world in new directions without being a burden in some lives," I suggested. "If you want to change the world, be prepared to make good trouble. If you study the lives of activists, I think you will find they made people uncomfortable." She told me she just might do that.

When she told me she felt better and was no longer considering suicide, even though I wanted to hear more from this inspiring young woman, we ended the call.

If, in our few moments together, that young woman began to discover a sense of who she is, and who she might become, I was blessed to witness a budding John Lewis, Greta Thunberg, Stacey Abrams, or Malala Yousafzai. If, in my lifetime, I do nothing more than, as Neil Postman suggested, send that one message to a future I will not see, that is enough.

Part 2
New Perspectives

I love to ask people if they view their worlds differently than they did five, ten, or even twenty years ago. In almost every case, individuals, without a moment's hesitation, recall how much their world has shifted because of whatever life put in their path. And, once people begin to realize how much their worldview has shifted, I suggest that similar changes to their outlook just might be in store over the next few years.

I, too, feel as though there are few ways in which I see the world that have remained constant over my lifetime. What follows is not a biography, nor does it even begin to describe how dramatically the lenses through which I view the world have changed. My intention is to share a few of the thousands of moments that have transformed my worldview, and serve as an encouragement for you, the reader, or those you wish to help, to open your mind and heart to a new, potentially radically new, future available by "Seeing Another Way."

Chapter 19
The Better Angels of Our Nature

In my experience, no one feels profound self-disappointment or failure unless they are molded from a core of kindness, generosity, and humanity.

I return for a moment to the veteran in Chapter 6 who, having been pushed over an emotional edge waiting in line at a retail store, said cruel things to the woman behind him in line. Recall he referred to himself as a "horrible, evil person," when our conversation began. But, when I asked if he wished to be a person who regrets letting himself and the world down, or if he would rather be a person who acts without humanity and simply does not care, he said "I want to be the person who is deeply sorry."

Whenever I tell this story, no matter the composition of the audience, I will ask, "By show of hands, who in the room believes this young man is *not* a horrible, evil human being?" Having asked thousands of people, I do not recall a single person whose hand remained at their side. When I ask why everyone agrees he is not evil, the dominant perspective is that anyone who makes a mistake, rues their unfortunate actions, and vows to do better allows us to see a core of goodness within. As one high school student observed, a truly evil person is one who is blind to evil.

Despite our wish to be kind, gentle, generous people, and despite our most heroic efforts, each of us will fail to live up to our expectations of self, repeatedly. In those moments, it is helpful to recall Voltaire's admonition, "Perfect is the enemy of good." We can use moments of failure to define us as inadequate, horrible human beings, or allow them to give us unique insights into who we are, and who we wish to be.

The core of goodness grows through the mistakes we make, insights we gain, and the actions we take to reweave goodness in the world. Recall I also asked that newly minted veteran if he might be a wiser, kinder, and more generous human being than he was moments earlier. His response was, "It never occurred to me to think of it that way, but maybe I am." As Abraham Lincoln suggested, we can allow ourselves to be touched by the "better angels of our nature."

Not long after that call, I was having coffee with a young friend who struggled through high school. I knew him briefly as a child of friends but was reacquainted with him through Operation Snowball when he got to high school.

Because of the challenges he faced throughout his life, especially in high school, "holy words" had fallen into this young man's heart. A close friend passed away, he lost a classmate to suicide, and, because of his gentle, kind nature, he was the target of hateful and bitter bullying. Because of all he encountered, he had richer insights into the human journey than his peers. Since he and I often shared a ride home from Snowball weekends, I relished the opportunity to hear the insights he gained from three days of vulnerability and authenticity with hundreds of his peers and adults.

Why is it that people most deeply scarred by the trials of life end up with expectations for themselves that are difficult, even impossible, to meet? As we spoke over coffee he was still struggling mightily. As we spoke, he admitted he often feels himself to be evil. It broke my heart. The word "evil" would never reside in anyone's description of this young soul…save for his own.

As we spoke, I looked into his eyes and realized he could only witness a mistake as errant because he viewed the world through a heart molded of goodness. A person who is truly evil would not have eyes that could see evil, nor a heart that could feel it.

In the end, we are, after all, only human. As much as I endeavor to turn every moment into one of worth and value, I know I will fail often. But when we can witness failures as evidence of our humanness, and endeavor to redeem ourselves in the future, our capacity for compassion, generosity, and wisdom continues to expand. Those moments become proof of our growing goodness, not our inhumanity.

Our mistakes do not describe us or define our character. It is what we do because of our inevitable errors that point inexorably to the better angels of our nature.

Chapter 20
Asking for What We Need

"I have dug myself into a bottomless hole. There is no way out. It often feels as if ending my life is the easiest way forward," a college student explained. "I have fallen behind in every class and I am failing most. If I flunk out of college, my life is over anyway," he told me. As he detailed his assignments and pending due dates, it felt, even to me, daunting.

A favorite question I like to pose to anyone overwhelmed by life is, "Of all the things you are facing, what feels the worst? What in your life, at this moment, feels most onerous?" Often, if we can deal with the worst, other challenges ease immensely.

When I asked that student that question, he told me of a paper that was due the following day. Completing that, he told me, felt like scaling Mount Everest. "Do you have a good relationship with the professor?" I asked. "I do. I like her, and have a great deal of respect for her," he replied. "What might happen," I asked, "if you went to her office this afternoon and told her what you told me. Be honest and vulnerable. Tell her how you feel overwhelmed. Explain you really want to write the paper, but, if you hand it in on time, you simply cannot give the topic justice. Tell her you know there will be consequences but ask if she might offer a reprieve." The relief I could feel in his voice was palpable. "Yes, I have a sense she will!" he exclaimed. "I am going to do that right now."

Another student called to tell me, he too, felt the only way forward was to end his life, but the reasons were different and devastating. He came, it turns out, from a lengthy line of doctors. His father, grandfather and most of his uncles and aunts, were physicians. His parents made it clear medicine was his future as well. "I'm trying," he told me, "But I *hate* it! The thought of spending my life as a doctor is simply abhorrent. But my parents have made it abundantly clear, if I do not pursue medicine, they will cut me off. I will be left with nothing. If my choices are medicine or suicide, well…" he admitted.

"If you could design the future of your choice, what would it include?" I asked. "Improv," he shot back without a moment's hesitation. "Being on stage and challenged by the immediacy, intensity, and abundant joy of improv is where I come alive. It is who I am at my very core. I don't know if I can make a career of it, but if I never try, I will spend the rest of my life in agony, wondering if I could have." "Can I ask," I continued, "is there anyone in your family who understands? Someone who might advocate for you with your parents." After a short pause, he exclaimed, "My Aunt…my father's sister! She loves me, and she has always seen me for who I am, and more importantly, who I am not. I'll bet she would be my advocate. I am going to call her the minute we are through and ask her to have lunch with me. I cannot wait to see what she has to say. Thank you so much!"

Sometimes we just need to ask. One Snowball weekend I found myself in a small group discussing the vagaries of life, and what we have learned about how to deal with their slings and arrows. Often those arrows come at us in such numbers, there does not appear to be any movement that will enable us to dodge them.

As we spoke that afternoon, one of the adults began to speak. "A few years ago, I admitted to myself and the world, I was in a marriage I needed to leave. There was no 'me' in that relationship. I felt lost and alone," she began. "Going through a messy divorce left me exhausted. I not only had to deal with the lawyers, court dates, and emotional trauma, I still had to negotiate day-to-day life. Those were horrible years. For a long time, I resented the fact that those around me—family and friends—did not see how my life was crumbling. They never came to my aid. As lost and alone as I felt in the relationship, I felt even more isolated and overwhelmed once I left," she continued.

"One day I realized," she told us, "I expected everyone to know I was overwhelmed. 'They should know my pain and offer help,' I thought. But how could they, I had not told anyone of my pain, nor had I ever told anyone what I needed. I realized I had to ask for the help I required. Once I let the world know of my suffering and my needs, everyone, it seemed, came to my aid." She concluded her story by asking each of us to be more honest, more vulnerable, with those around us. "We don't ever want to lay bare our weaknesses and the things we think are our failings, but, unless and until we do, how can we expect the world to know what we need in order to discover our wholeness?"

Asking for help is simple, and yet it fills us with fear. Asking for help, especially from those from whom we want love and respect, calls us to a kind of honesty for which we have little or no practice. Often, the help we need is right at hand, but we simply fail to see it.

Archbishop Desmond Tutu often reminded us that, to eat an elephant, you begin one bite at a time. When life feels overwhelming, ask what feels the worst. No one can do everything, but if we begin somewhere, deal with the worst, and remember to ask for what we need, the road ahead is shorter, and the twists and turns appear less treacherous.

Chapter 21
Thinking from the Heart

I have spoken before larger audiences, but this was to be my first TEDx talk. Giving such a talk is a huge honor. However, at some point you realize your remarks will live on the Internet forever; it matters not whether you deliver them with eloquence…or stumble meaninglessly for 18 minutes. The thought of reliving a mediocre performance for the rest of one's life can add a certain amount of terror to the moment.

As I drafted, edited, and practiced my remarks, my hope was to influence those who might eventually hear them. I had three or four groups willing to hear what was on my mind in the weeks preceding TEDxIIT, so I had abundant opportunities to rehearse and rewrite the message. I learned an important lesson. Whenever I edged towards a logical, rational narration, the audience responded with polite applause and kind comments. When I spoke from my heart, with words tinted by emotion, those to whom I spoke reacted with rapt attention and walked away with deeper understanding. They found within, and shared with each other, more profound wisdom.

John Keats once said the heart is the only organ strong enough to educate the mind. When improvisational pianist Michael Jones reminded me of Keats' wisdom, he added, "When we are thinking from our heart, we are never far from tears."

The journey I traversed in the 24 hours before my walk onto that stage is worth a moment so I can honor the person who gave me permission to think from my heart…to navigate the territory between logic and emotion with deep authenticity in that very public, frightening place.

The fourteen presenters rehearsed the day before TEDxIIT. After my rehearsal, Bob, the stage manager and advisor, pulled me aside and admitted my remarks touched him. Bob is a professional speaker and actor—his command of the stage is inspiring—so his generous comment helped build my confidence and allay the terror. However, as the conference began the following day, my trepidation grew. Since the talks preceding mine had a decidedly technical bent, I feared the audience would be uninterested in my message. I intended my remarks to educate their mind by touching their hearts.

At the break, I told Bob I was losing my nerve. When I expressed fear the audience was in a state of mind rather than a state of heart, he said, "What you have to say is more important than any of the technology stuff." It was kind and generous, but not as powerful as the words he imparted in the "Green Room" a moment before I walked on the stage. He grabbed my arm, looked me in the eye, and said, "Go out there and make me cry!"

From the first moments on that stage, as I mentioned my work on the suicide hotline, I wrestled with tears. I wondered if I touched on my emotions too early, but as I walked off the stage, Bob reassured me once again. "Did you see the audience's reaction? You grabbed their attention from those early moments and never let go."

I frequently find myself betwixt and between logical thought and deep emotion; caught somewhere in the fissure between my cerebral cortex and my heart. We live in an era that would have us believe the logical and rational are the singular keys to success. We practically abhor emotions. When they arrive, often unbidden, the culture encourages us not to feel.

The word courage and the word heart both derive from the Latin word *cor*. It takes courage to allow the heart to educate the mind. Someday, I hope, we will become more comfortable thinking from our hearts…and honor those who are never far from tears.

Chapter 22
To Look Again

I can only imagine how difficult it must be to be a police officer. I do not doubt that some officers disgrace the badge they wear and fail in their call to serve and protect. However, I have known many for whom I have tremendous respect.

Whenever a call to the suicide hotline ended unsuccessfully—we believed the caller was still in danger when the phones disconnected—we relied on first responders to find the person and get them help. Only once, in 20 years, did I have the privilege of listening in the moments after the first responders arrived. When that call began, the caller, feeling unsafe, asked me to call the police and have them take him to an emergency room and asked me to stay on the phone until the first responders arrived. To my surprise, he did not end the call when the police arrived. I was honored to hear what the officers said in the ensuing moments. I was in tears as I heard the kind and gentle words used with this man. They were caring, thoughtful, and genuinely interested in learning what this man faced and why he was thinking of ending his life. As soon as the call disconnected, I called the station from which these officers were dispatched to express my profound gratitude. How fortunate to have such officers serving and protecting.

Because officers deal everyday with citizens who subvert the law, they are witness to the brutal underbelly of society. It is no wonder, after years of encountering the worst, officers can become jaded in their view of others. It is no surprise that these servants, as a group, face one of the highest suicide rates of any profession.

In 2007 and 2008, the town in which I live lost two officers to suicide. I, as well as anyone, understand that asking our first responders to wear so many different hats—from ending violent crime, to protecting neighborhoods, and acting as counselors and social workers—is untenable. Innovative solutions must be explored and implemented. However, to the hundreds of thousands of police officers who struggle every day to serve and protect, I offer these few words of honor.

> *It is too late to thank two officers, who, for reasons we will never fully understand, found their lives so unbearable that they chose to end them.*
>
> *In the wake of their deaths, I have been thinking about ways I silently mistreat the men and women whose lives revolve around the simple pledge to "serve and protect." In fulfilling this sacred oath, they find themselves in the position of interrupting the normal flow of life—stopping me for a violation or redirecting a trip home to deliver me safely past an accident or construction project. And when that interruption impacts my life, they are too often the recipients of my frustration and anger.*
>
> *Years ago, I spent time with an officer in his patrol car. In those hours, there wasn't an opportunity for anyone to affirm him for his work. In fact, since his time was spent inserting himself between the lawful and unlawful sides of our society—facing only the unlawful side—I could not imagine when a kind word or a simple thank you would be part of his job. These servants typically face only danger, sadness, and criticism. They halt dangerous practices in the community, end domestic disputes, and wake us in the middle of the night when a loved one is lost to one of life's tragedies. We have even come to rely on them to resolve*

neighborhood disagreements we have become too timid to face personally.

The word respect is based on a root that means to look. Respect means to "look again." We respect another when we take off our blinders—reflect on our biases and limited interpretations of life—and look with fresh eyes at who they really are. Since we lost two officers to suicide, I have been trying to show my respect for the men and women of the Police Department by looking again at the things they do to make this community a safe and magnificent place to live.

I am, again, reminded that the way I often see the world is only one perspective. When I allow myself to see with new eyes, there is another way to see.[6]

[6] I recently read *My Grandmother's Hands: Racialized Trauma and the Pathway to Mending Our Hearts and Bodies* by Resmaa Menakem. His work gave me great insight into the role of police in communities of color. I realize that many officers in those communities are not viewed as servants or protectors. He delves deeply into ways in which that might change. My hope is that his experience and wisdom might help in the near future.

Chapter 23
Beware Your Expectations

"Why would you leave the stage in the middle of a song?"

From the Song "Why" by Rascal Flatts

Occasionally, I am arrogant enough to think that life has left me in charge. Whenever I feel that way, life is quick to remind me I am not.

After the Operation Snowball family lost another teen to suicide, the teen directors decided to use the weekly Thursday evening meeting to explore the scourge of teen suicide. They chose two videos and asked me to facilitate the ensuing discussion.

I watched the videos that afternoon. They were compelling. The second one was based on the song "Why," by the country music group Rascal Flatts. The line quoted above rips my heart out every time I hear that gut-wrenching piece of music.

All afternoon, I held tight as I rode an emotional roller coaster imagining the powerful evening that might emerge. In my hands would be the hearts and minds of fifty or more teens. These extraordinary young people meant so much to me, the possibility of turning these few sacred moments into a deep learning experience—one in which they might look inside and glimpse a bit of their radiance—was overwhelming.

I contemplated what I might say...the stories I might tell... and the tears and emotions that would surely show them the depth of my care and concern. I recalled a metaphor from Thich Nhat Hanh in which the master gardener could see flowers amid compost. I searched for the perfect reflections from Dr. Rachel Remen, who, in the course of her work with those dying of cancer, discovered the power and meaning that can emerge even from life's most challenging moments. I even brought words that flowed from my heart in the aftermath of the death of other teens I had known. I recounted, in my head, hundreds of ways these words and stories might help the teens peer into their own lives, even with the moments of excruciating pain and heartache, and glimpse the insight and wisdom available on the other side of the journey into hell.

The teens come to the Thursday night meetings to reconnect over games, experiences, and exercises, most of which are fun. To expect them to spend a precious evening on a difficult, emotional topic is a great deal to ask. The least I could give them is insight into the meaning of life. Some small awakening that might be adequate compensation for a somber evening. That wisdom was inside me; I felt it welling up as the evening approached.

But life had another lesson in store. It was not I who was in charge, but the teens who came to share their stories.

The tears and emotions that would show the depth of my love and concern were simply unavailable that evening. The stories I was certain would emerge unbidden, were elusive. The wisdom I knew I could share remained locked inside, unavailable when I needed it most. I went home devastated. I felt as though I had let the participants down. Even worse, I let down the teen directors who have so much respect for me that they entrusted me with these moments. At the very least I let myself down.

I realize now, I wasted my own evening, spending too much of our time contemplating the value of my contribution, missing the wisdom and insight brought to the discussion through the life, experience, and wisdom of the teens at Operation Snowball. The teens shared their stories and brought forth their wisdom. It was a powerful evening, with each teen leaving with precisely the lessons they needed.

Expectations are a fickle master. They grab hold of us, drag us in the direction of their choosing, and do not give a whit about what the world truly needs. Whenever expectations attempt to control my future, I try to remember the words of the Irish poet, John O'Donohue: "Expectations are resentments under construction."

Chapter 24
Orchids and Roses

One weekend just before Thanksgiving, my wife and I joined our children in a neighboring community for a family tradition of attending a variety of pre-holiday events.

All weekend, the two of us sat in amazement in the presence of our children. I knew they were no more amazing than millions of other emerging young adults, but since they are my children, I demanded the right to be in awe of who they were becoming and speak of them as if they truly are God's gift…because to me they are.

After expressing my amazement on social media, a friend commented, in part, "Everything you and your wife did explains their beauty." I appreciate the generosity, but it is difficult for me to see how my efforts—occasionally kind, gentle and loving, but often tinged by personal struggles and imperfections—could explain the beauty in front of me that weekend. As hard as I tried, as much as I wished to be a perfect parent, I grieve the endless times I failed; the hundreds of times they longed for a listening and compassionate ear, and I found it necessary instead to attempt to fix or teach. I lament how the stresses of my life intruded on theirs in the form of unjustified anger and frustration. I mourn the lost opportunities when a different kind of attention would have nourished them in more abundant ways. And yet, despite my failings, they emerge as caring, compassionate, fervent adults.

My wife has a growing passion, and a passion for growing, orchids. After more than a year, she coaxed one of her plants into rewarding us with three gorgeous blooms. They were stunning. And while I do not want to demean the loving care she gave them, their beauty is far greater than the effort to foster it. A bit of care, water and a nourishing environment yielded a thing of stunning beauty. The orchid rushes forth, becoming what it was always intended to be so long as it has a healthy environment, and nothing gets in the way of its journey from seed to blossom. The magnificence of the blossom is contained in the tiny seed from which it grows. No matter how hard she might have tried, no matter the extent of her care or the nourishment she provided, she could not coax the plant into producing roses. Anything she might have tried would surely have damaged this thing of beauty.

When people tell us we did a wonderful job raising our children, I usually reflect that if we did anything well, we stayed out of their way just enough. We tried to provide a loving, nourishing environment, but we always knew they would blossom into the amazing humans they were intended to become—an orchid if it was their birthright or a rose if that is what was implanted in their soul.

So why have I been given the gifts of my children? Just maybe, they were not put here for me to be the teacher, but the learner.

Chapter 25
Living the Messages of Others

Whenever I recall Neil Postman's insightful reminder that children are the messages we send to a time we will not see, I am reminded of my own mortality. There will be, in what seem like the briefest of moments, a time I will not see.

None of us will be remembered. My children, and a few of their friends, will remember me, as will the next generation, albeit with far less intensity. If I am remembered a third or fourth generation hence, it will be at most in wisps…an occasional anecdote, image, or memory. Beyond that I am quite certain the human whose moniker was Roger Breisch will be forgotten.

But Postman reminds me of a different kind of immortality. Any time humans imprint wisdom upon one another, each moves into the future carrying the messages learned from the other. Thoughts change, actions change, and the future becomes something new. When we have the unique opportunity to touch the lives of children and young adults, there is the possibility some small piece of us will live into a more distant—and different—future. That thought brings tears to my eyes when a teen at Snowball, or a person on the suicide hotline, admits to having a new thought or understanding because of our connection.

But that view puts me at the center, as progenitor of messages to the future. What if I am not?

When I attended my 45th high school reunion, I discovered that Ed Deyman, a classmate, had reproduced with pen & ink all 250 portraits from our senior yearbook. From the moment I saw mine, I was astonished how well Ed captured the young man I was those many years ago. When I returned home, I unfurled the portrait on the kitchen counter. I was struck by how the eyes followed me regardless of the angle from which I tried to elude them.

Weeks later, the ink on paper suddenly came to life. As I peered with more care and a bit of compassion, it was no longer simply a sketch on the counter—the person I knew so intimately for the first 18 years of his life was staring at me. It was an unexpected moment of intimacy between two people who knew one another well, but each had somehow forgotten the other existed.

The eyes on that portrait peered deeply into my soul. It was as if that young man could see me, the man he was to become, in the same way I could see him. He was able to examine the life he was to live. I could hold nothing back, since he would see every moment of joy and grace, and live every mistake, from the minuscule to those that remain intensely painful.

For a year, that portrait lay on the counter staring at me expectantly. I struggled to discern what it might be asking.

Then, one day, it came to me. Just as today, I show up in the lives of young people with as much authenticity as I can so they might discern a message that fits their lives, in the years since that image was captured, there have been hundreds of adults whose lives taught me something unique about what it means to be human. "Are we," that young man is asking me, "living with integrity, sincerity and love into the messages those extraordinary humans formed within us?"

I approached junior year in high school with a fair amount of math success on my brief resume. I loved geometry, and, while algebra was not my favorite, I managed reasonable grades. But as I approached my third year of high school, I was about to face, not only trigonometry, but one of the teachers every student feared, Sister Anne.

I soon discovered the most fearsome thing about Sister Anne was that she had lofty expectations and was not about to compromise. She believed in us and cared deeply about our success. And while my trepidation remained, especially before exams, it eased greatly as I discovered I was, often, able to live up to her expectations.

But no amount of success could prepare me for one pivotal day during my senior year.

We had a small class of fourth-year math students. Because we were the few who agreed to test our mettle against the most advanced math class, Sister Anne raised her expectations even higher. She devised a truly terrifying challenge. She assigned each of us a complex mathematical topic, unrelated to the fourth-year syllabus. She told us we were not only to research the topic, but to hone our understanding so exquisitely that we could present it coherently to the rest of the class.

I have no recollection of the topic I was assigned, but I remember sitting in the library, staring blankly into texts that held my future. I read and reread the words, but understanding eluded me for what seemed like hours. I felt lost and very alone.

I can still recall—even re-feel—the moment of elation when the shroud lowered. The euphoria emanated, not from a cursory understanding, but from a deep sense of comprehension. I could not wait to share my excitement with my classmates.

So, we come to the day Sister Anne helped me see myself in a new way. Those moments, standing next to the overhead projector (yes, it was a *long* time ago!), tendered a sense of joy I had never experienced. In those moments, a facility arose in me; I found myself turning complexity into simplicity. It felt magical.

In those few moments, I discovered the teacher within. In every talk I give, every word I write, I strive to turn complexity into simplicity. My goal is to help others understand something that may have eluded them. There is a bit of Sister Anne in everything I do. Surely Sister Anne played a role years later as I and my own students struggled to "see it another way." She exists in all the stories that make up this volume.

46 years after graduation, as I recalled the message she sent into the world through me, I was sad I never told her how she changed my life. Until, thanks to social media, a classmate told me Sister Anne was living and working in Michigan. I called her and had an opportunity to tell her how she changed my life. It filled my heart with joy. It turns out, this amazing woman, founded a new religious order, and eventually returned to school to get a law degree and spent twenty years fighting on behalf of the abused, poor, and underprivileged.

Another teacher arrived in my life during my junior year in high school. As a Catholic school, we were required to take religion classes every year. Most were very traditional. That year, however, my life was upended in the class taught by Fr. LaGoe. Fr. LaGoe had a reputation for strident and unorthodox views. Of all the views considered controversial, his was as close to being radically antiracist as anyone I could imagine. In our classes, we spent a great deal of time talking about racial issues, significant people of the time, and the events taking place around the country. I can still hear the sadness in his voice, and the pained look on his face during those discussions. It did not have the moniker at the time, but

Fr. LaGoe provided us with an advanced degree in Critical Race Theory, and I am ever so grateful.

I was in his class on April 5, 1968, the day after Dr. Martin Luther King, Jr. was assassinated. It was Fr. LaGoe's influence that encouraged me to read books about racial issues. He started me on a learning journey, my own personal journey into Critical Race Theory that continues to this day.

In the world I now discern, I am the carrier of their messages, as well as those of thousands of others, more than I am the progenitor of my own. It is humbling to remember I am simply the medium through which their wisdom is gifted to the future. If, along the way, I add a small bit of insight to theirs, then I too will live into untold generations yet unborn.

As I live day-to-day, it is difficult to always recall the impact so many have had on my life. But, I will try, with integrity, sincerity, and love, to be the living messages each hoped I would carry into a time they no longer see.

Chapter 26
Being A Hole in the Flute

Even at the quantum level, as separate and distinct, a single particle has little value. It is only when they are in relationship with other quantum entities that they form the universe. So too for humanity. Absent our intimate relationships—deep connections—with all things, even those we call inanimate, we are nothing.

As I write, since I feel my fingers on the keyboard, I imagine the computer and I as separate and distinct. However, if I were to pick up a writing instrument to pen these same words, the experience and result would be different. The computer and I co-create. My relationship to even the most inanimate of objects alters the future.

As I trek through the woods, a tree ahead appears distinct from me. I know where my body "ends" and the leaves, branches, and trunk "begin." But do I? There is a symbiotic relationship between us. The oxygen I inhale in this moment was "exhaled" by that living organism moments ago. The carbon dioxide I release into the atmosphere is vital to the tree's future. Each season, a tree will take thousands of gallons of water from the soil and release it into the air as water vapor. Those molecules return to Earth as rain, and to me through the foods I eat and the water I drink. The tree and I are in deep relationship; I am biologically part of that tree, and it is a part of me.

Even thoughts originating in my cerebral cortex, which my ego insists make me distinct from others, are proof of relationship not separation. Every neural pathway in my brain was formed through experience with, and mental formulations that originate in, the world outside of me. Every sound I hear, article I touch, morsel I taste and object I see, alters my relationship with the world and changes the entity I thought myself to be.

My emotional being, as well, is intimately related to, and formed by, the world around me. Every story of pain and heartache I encounter in the lives of friends, or from a call on the suicide hotline, alters my emotional sense of the world.

There is little we own…little for which we can take credit. Every word, every thought, every feeling, emerges from ideas and experiences gifted to us by others. Nor is our ability to hold, synthesize and retell them ours to own. They, too, are gifts we have learned from others.

If I search deeply for the "I" I believe is me, I soon discover there isn't one. The harder I look, the more intense my gaze, the more I discover that everything I think of as me, was formed through an infinity of relationships. I am nothing more than a confluence of influences; simply the intersection of the fields through which this collection of human cells has traveled. I am, simply put, the result of trillions of quantum particles in relationship.

Western culture moves in harmony with the sacredness and importance of the individual. We go to any lengths, and put people in jeopardy, to save one. But the moment I drift from the sacredness of life to the importance of my own, I excise myself from humanity. I allow myself to become isolated; distinct and apart. My thoughts and ideas are wrenched from their rightful place within the ecosystem where they formed, and where they can be challenged, debated, refined, and potentially discarded. Ego takes over and I elevate my ideas to a place of superiority and rightness.

The Sufi mystic and poet Hafitz once said "I am a hole in the flute through which God's breath flows." At best, the confluence of thoughts, ideas, and experiences I refer to as myself is no more than a capacity through which the Universe itself is trying to be seen. If I can remain true to simply being the hole, and refrain from imagining myself to be the breath, or the player of the flute, only then is there hope.

Chapter 27
The Universe Rearranging Itself

"At the deepest level, there is no giver, no gift, and no recipient…only the universe rearranging itself."

Jon Kabat-Zinn

Beauty is in the eye of the beholder. So too are gifts. I have learned this in many ways, but none more poignant than the hundreds of heart-wrenching moments spent on the suicide hotline with those whose lives became so difficult they contemplated ending them. In those moments, it is easy to mistake the gifts, who gives them, and who receives them.

A major portion of training for suicide intervention involves learning how to gently enter a conversation by taking time to connect deeply with the caller, trying to understand what it is about their life that makes it so unbearable. Through deep listening, empathy, and our natural human ability to truly converse, we build a relationship that allows us, at some sacred moment, to discern why the person has persevered to this moment. Is there a reason they want to live?

It is in the ensuing moments that a space opens for a human heart to burst open. A young father in tears says, "I have the most beautiful children in the world. How could I ever hurt them? Another will admit "My parents love me so much. If I ended my life, a part of theirs too would end." Or the person at the other end has already given so much of themselves that they are physically, financially, and emotionally drained, and yet they say, "I know I still have much to give to the world." Sometimes a caller will burst into tears and simply exclaim "I don't want to die!" In those sacred moments it is not only the person's heart in which a fissure appears…hearts at both ends of the conversation open to one another. My own tears remind me of my humanity…and gratitude for life.

When I trained new volunteers, they would listen in on calls as I spent time with humans in need. After one difficult, emotionally draining call, a trainee said, "Roger, you have a gift." It was a wonderful, generous thing to say, but if she meant that I have a unique ability, I must demure. It is the essence of what it means to be human to sit with another in their moment of sorrow, pain and hurt, and simply listen. We all have that gift, even if some may have forgotten how to offer it.

Often, after a particularly difficult call—a voyage from treacherous, stormy waters roiled by thoughts of death to a sea ever-so-slightly calmed by a renewed desire for life—a person will express gratitude for our time together. I will sometimes, in return, tell my fellow voyagers they were a gift in my life. It takes them by surprise, and many do not believe me. But during our journey they may have reminded me of the life-affirming power of the love between parents and children…or the profundity of the human desire to cling to life…or the elegance and beauty of simple human connection. I am, during those moments, fully immersed in the vulnerable, raw, and revealing human condition. It is not possible to take such a journey and return untouched.

Today, I am invited into numerous high schools to talk with teenage students about the lessons and gifts I received for 20 years and more than 11,000 phone calls. The students often ask how I might have been changed by listening to the suffering of others. I tell them that, despite the harrowing emotional journeys I have traveled with others, the emotion I felt, more than any other, at the end of a shift is gratitude. I tell the story of the young man with a gun cradled in his lap, who was ready to end his life at the end of our call. "When a young man calls with the intention of ending his life, and at the end of our time together, he puts the gun away and chooses to see value in himself he did not see when he called, how could I feel anything but gratitude and grace in the face of his courage?"

At the end of one long day speaking to eight sophomore health classes, the teacher escorting me to my car remarked how engaged her eighth period class was. "You have a gift," she said as we approached my car. In the moments since I heard her kind and generous observation, I have recalled the gifts I have received over the years from young people who have told me of the insights they gained from our time together.

One student shared this insight:

> *I would like to thank you for the presentation. You revealed that the real heroes of our society are hidden from us and don't get the attention and recognition that they deserve. My life's goal is to leave the world a better place than when I got to it, thus I thought I needed to do something huge to reach this goal, … to "change" the world. But you showed it is possible to do that just by showing love, kindness, and care to people. You saved lives, and you didn't even know if they were "bad" or "good" people. I think it is because, as you said, you see great things in everybody.*

Another sent this bit of wisdom:

> *Dealing with other's life or death must be a huge responsibility. You are one of the bravest men that I have ever seen. You said we must be genuine for others to know we care. I want to let you know that I do. Thank you for letting me see that in myself.*

After one presentation, a student approached me to express appreciation for my words, and that he was certain many of his classmates felt the same. I told him his words were a gift in my life. "At my age," I reflected, "the idea that I can find messages that have meaning to a room filled by people two or three generations younger than I, fills me with joy and gratitude."

In so many moments during the brief journey that is my life, the Universe has rearranged itself frequently in my presence, and I feel far more the recipient of gifts and grace than the giver.

Chapter 28
Feeling Beautifully Incomplete

"Finally I see…life has been patiently waiting for me."

From the song "I'm Movin' On" by Rascal Flatts.

It was not a new thought…I had heard it expressed as "When the student is ready, the teacher appears." But in an instant, I remembered that our lives do not show up until we are ready to truly listen, see and experience.

The song "I'm Movin' On" and I had simultaneously visited the same space many times, but being in the same place with an idea or a person does not mean you are friends…or even acknowledge one another's presence. It certainly does not mean you are in love. But one morning, on the way to a local coffee shop, I began a love affair with the words "life has been patiently waiting for me." I have learned to listen carefully when words touch my heart, and these—in that moment—surely did.

The more I reflected on them, the more hopeful, valued and beautifully incomplete I felt. The *hope* came from the sudden sense that it was okay, even as I bid adieu to middle age and entered elderhood, that life was still willing to wait for me. I had not missed my opportunity yet. I felt *valued* because I was important enough to be waited for, and I wasn't being waited for by something insignificant—I was being waited for by life itself! Finally, I felt *beautifully incomplete*! Yes, beautifully incomplete. To be complete would be to imply that there was nothing left to life. Nothing left to learn. No one left for me to touch, or to be touched by. Life still held the promise of much to learn, new experiences, and people yet to touch. Incomplete never felt so wonderful.

The words filled the car and, for whatever reason, they meant something new. The older I get, the more I realize that life is less about doing, and more about being ready for the teacher...and that the teacher waits patiently everywhere and in every moment. Waits patiently for me.

However, the question that really captured me, as I thought about life waiting patiently for me, is this...who is the me life is waiting patiently for? If I am incomplete, are there parts of me nearing completion? Are there parts I have yet to even begin to know? If I "know" many things about who I am, am I certain which are real and which are imposters? How, over the course of my lifetime have I learned to tell the real from the false...the identities that are me, versus those my ego inappropriately apprehended and is unwilling to release? There seemed to be an endless series of questions that arose from "who is the me that life is waiting for?"

The more I thought about it, the more I realized that it raised an even more profound question. Is the "me" life is waiting for something I have within my power to create, like sculptors fashion form out of amorphous clay or stone, or something that already exists for me to reveal, as a landscape is revealed when curtains are gently parted? As those words—life has been patiently waiting for me—pierced my psyche, I began to wonder if the highest purpose of my life here on Earth is to live into—to fully inhabit—a life that is itself, waiting for me.

I wonder if a common vision of human life—the pervasive Western view—is somehow skewed, perhaps even backward. I was raised to believe that humans are born *tabula rasa*—we arrive as a clean slate on which our story is written and that we are the primary authors. Born as nothing more than potential, we are given untold years on this Earth during which to create ourselves. "You can be whatever you want to be," I was told in so many ways…and by so many people. The evidence they use to prove that life works this way can be compelling. Look at the legions of role models whose lives seem to verify the worldview—the millions of politicians, entrepreneurs, religious leaders, and community organizers to whom we frequently point, who made something of themselves. The story line is that through their effort they made themselves into something they would not have been if they had not carefully sculpted it from an amorphous presence.

I am no longer certain that life works that way. I find that I have become—and continue to grow into—a human being different from any I ever imagined. Certainly not the one I would have set out to sculpt. I was destined, I imagined in an earlier life, for something big! A captain of industry. Well-respected, even adorning the cover of a respected magazine.

But I am discovering that I am in fact big, but in ways people would consider small. I spent intense moments with those who live at the desperate end of a suicide hotline, helping them find reasons to live. I was, for ten years, "captain" of industry in the small town that knew me as Executive Director of the Chamber of Commerce where I spent my days helping entrepreneurs achieve their dreams. I spent most Thursday nights, and two weekends each year, with teens in Operation Snowball, encouraging them to discern lifestyles filled by life, in a world where they face so many who choose self-destruction. My story—a story filled with more joy than I could ever have imagined—feels like a life I discovered, not one I created.

So, what is that story? It is a story of emergence more than one of creation. I wonder if life is about growing into who we are meant to be rather than creating who we wish to become.

I wonder if life is about allowing the core of who we are to emerge. Taking a metaphor from nature, an oak tree emerges—it does not create itself. A rose blossoms, it does not endeavor to be something other than what it is destined to become.

The image I have in mind is that Roger Breisch has, and has had since conception, unique, powerful, and specific strengths…characteristics…personality traits…gifts. The perfect descriptor escapes me. But what is important is that the quality of my impact on the world is in direct relation to the extent to which I show up through those gifts—naked and authentic. To the extent I insist on showing up without them, to the extent I try to create a world as someone I am not, I am lost, ineffective and superficial.

Mahatma Gandhi began as a fiery lawyer but altered the future of mankind only after he discovered that the true spark within was ignited through patience, civil disobedience, and peaceful protest. Nelson Mandela went to prison for his passionate, radical self, but touched the heart of the world when he discovered his wise, thoughtful, peaceful nature. Early in their lives they tried to create themselves into someone they felt could change the world, only to discover later in life the person who truly could…and did.

As I listened to Rascal Flatts that morning I began to wonder how I might be becoming the person life is waiting patiently for.

As I answer calls on the suicide hotline, I feel helpful when I apply the techniques taught in training, but I feel meaningful when I show up with those pieces of myself into which I have begun to grow. When a piece of me intermingles with a raw and tender facet of a caller, we end our time together and both of us are changed. They give me the gift of discovering who I am and of what I am capable—more than anything I may have given them.

In his best-selling book, *The Soul's Code* psychologist James Hillman expounds on his acorn theory. "This theory states that everyone holds the potential for their unique possibilities inside themselves, just as an acorn holds the pattern for an oak tree. It describes how a unique energy is contained within each human being, and is displayed throughout their lifetime, and shown in their calling and life's work when it is fully blossomed or actualized." Hillman suggests that we enter life with an agenda, something we need to accomplish during the next portion of our journey, and we are born into a life that gives us the greatest potential to complete that plan.

What I am suggesting is that who I am—the gifts I have to offer, the way in which I see and experience the world—is waiting to be discovered by me, and, the effect I have on the world is far more potent if what I do, and what I become, is deeply informed by that unique creature for whom life is waiting.

There is a different way of seeing the sculptor…different from one who creates. I have heard it said that, in speaking of his magnificent sculpture of David, Michelangelo was asked how he could find David within a simple, amorphous block of stone. He said the task was easy…he simply chipped away the parts that did not look like David. That is an image of discovery, not one of creation. That is a more powerful way of envisioning our lives. As we grow, we become what others want us to be in return for the sustenance and love we need for survival. Midlife crisis, one Jungian suggested, is the sudden discovery that the person we have become is not who we really are, nor wish to be. Life then becomes a process of chipping away the parts of the stone we have become that no longer look like—or feel like—us.

A Mathematician Sees Another Way

Within these pages, I have tried to introduce you to people in my life—self included—who viewed their lives inaccurately and incompletely. For too many, not witnessing their sense of self another way, led to a choice to end lives that were brilliant, generous, and filled with potential. For others, had they not found the courage to see themselves in another way, they may have chosen a similar tragic end.

Could we see life another way? The answer, after recalling hundreds of episodes that have informed my life, is yes we can. But I believe it to be the wrong question. Now, in my eighth decade, I have come to see that a more appropriate and pressing question is, can we afford *not* to see it in a different way? I am just as emphatic when I say the answer is a definitive, confrontational, deafening, "No!"

But the world we inhabit is so much more than the stories of more than eight billion members of the species *Homo sapiens.* While we are a sliver of this unique biosphere, our impact far exceeds anything we may believe is our right. If we choose not to see our actions and their consequences in other ways, I fear for the future of our species. In another work[7], I explored a hopeful future in which our species becomes compassionate, generous, and grateful members of this fragile, magnificent planet.

One of the first languages in which I felt fluent was that of Mathematics. In many respects, that language seems incongruous with the life I have described in the preceding pages. Afterall, Mathematics can be viewed as pure logic in which "truth" is black or white. With a few exceptions at its

---

[7] "Humanity's Journey Home: Surrendering to the Wholeness that is Gaia" by Roger Breisch, 2021

edges, a question asked is proven either true or false. There appear to be few, if any, grey areas. It is through that lens that I often see the world. It comes as no surprise my children once gave me the moniker "Funsucker." "Dad," they will say, sometimes, but not always, in jest, "you always see why things *won't* work. That sucks the fun out of everything!" Guilty as charged!

While I have yet to use an algebraic formulation or geometric proof in any of the episodic adventures that have defined my life, there is a way of thinking, a way of untangling knotty problems, that has been the bedrock of thousands of discussions with people in their moment of grief, depression, and confusion. If I have listened carefully, I can often help them recall something that helps them see their life in a new way:

- The person who lived a life of unfair and appalling abuse, calling the Lifeline with a gun in his lap, was able to see the abuse gifted him with a huge and compassionate heart he was using to save the lives of other young men.
- The neuroscientist who believed his life had to include major discoveries, realized his love of the violin, pointed to a life of "smaller," yet invaluable, contributions.
- The young woman suffering from anxiety and clinical depression, who was certain she had to leave a loving relationship for the benefit of her partner, began to see that her love for him was so deep, it was, truly enough.
- The actor whose thespian path forward was lacking, only to discover he was, at his core, other-centered.

Similarly, the young man changing the lives of other aspiring drag queens.

- The veteran, thinking himself an evil individual, came to see his core as a caring and good young man.
- The man reemployed at a much-reduced salary, certain he failed his family, realized the value of his love far outweighed the size of his bank accounts.
- The three perfectionists who, after realizing that perfect is the enemy of good, saw a new path forward.

Having studied everything from Algebra, Geometry, Trigonometry, and Calculus to Abstract Algebra, Topology, and Real and Complex Analysis, I understand how those areas of mathematics flow from the assumptions we make. Euclidian Geometry rests on the assumption that, given a line and a point not on the line, there is one and only one line through that point parallel to the line. Remaining vigilant to Euclidean Geometry has allowed *Homo sapiens* to create the world we experience. However, for Einstein's Theory of Relativity to exist, we must yield that assumption. It seems strange and counterintuitive, but yield, we must.

The assumptions we allow, and those we refuse, not only change Mathematics, but have much to do with the outcomes of our lives.

Recall the stories in which people allowed questionable personal or societal assumptions to rule their lives, and blind them to a new, more beautiful future.

- Parents whose assumptions about, and for, their children made deep listening and true understanding impossible.

- Elders who have not shared their lives with future generations because "they don't want to burden them with my problems."
- The young, mostly women, who thought the abuse in their relationships was a sign of care and love.
- The assumptions so many of us carry about those who are other-abled as opposed to disabled.
- Dakota who could see beauty in everyone except himself.
- The assumptions we have about mental illness that leave those who suffer feeling weak and engulfed with guilt.
- Our belief that pain is to be feared, rejected, and hidden, rather than accepted and fully embraced to reduce its devastating grip.

Those thoughts describe how the logical mathematician has shown up in my time with others. However, there is another side of me I do not understand, even to this day. That side has to do with tears. Like my father, who hated the arrival of his own, they come to me unexpectedly and unbidden. I, too, find it embarrassing, but I have endeavored to come to know and honor them. If you ask students who know me at Snowball, they will tell you one of the things they love about me is my willingness to be open, authentic, and vulnerable, and that includes revealing that men can show tears.

One particular moment on a Snowball weekend changed me. The final event on Sunday is a hug circle in which every participant gives and receives hugs from every other. On that weekend, I completed all the requisite embraces a bit early. There was a young man, also finished, standing near me. I had not met him during the weekend, so I approached and asked what he learned about himself in the preceding days. "I learned that I cry easily," he replied. Knowing how important my tears are at Snowball, I pointed to his heart and suggested that his willingness to be vulnerable just might be his superpower. In that moment, he told me, he understood a young black man could put down his macho mask, even for a moment. He became overwhelmed, put his arms around me, and held on as if his life depended on it. That tear-filled embrace lasted a long time. It is a hug I will never forget.

Those two sides—the logician and empath—have found a way to coexist within me. I cannot say I understand the relationship between them, and I have learned to allow each of them to show up when needed. I learned I am not in control.

Finally, I return one last time to the lesson I learned from the young, budding mathematicians I encountered as an inexperienced teacher. Could we see another way? How can we not? These questions have animated much of my life. Their impact comes through each of the episodes of my life and is the way of this mathematician. It has allowed me to discern wisdom held by thousands. And if, even in some small way, you have been touched by those who touched me, your perspective has been altered. Together, we have altered initial conditions in this moment, and, given the butterfly effect, the course of human history has been irrevocably altered.

Thank you.

www.ingramcontent.com/pod-product-compliance
Lightning Source LLC
LaVergne TN
LVHW050822061126
851857LV00012B/925
9798234137180